THE REAL TRUTH ABOUT GETTING A JOB

Uncloaking the Myths, Facing the Realities
Understanding New Paradigms

By Dayton E. Conway

Aurora, Colorado

August 2012

Dedication

To Will Hiltscher

The finest engineer I know

and to

Jackie Collins

Her character is unparalleled

Table of Contents.

Forward: Why you will want to read this book.	7
Chapter One: The game – what it's all about	9
Chapter Two: Good jobs, bad jobs	16
Chapter Three: Assaulting the fairy castle	37
Chapter Four: People-charging your campaign	47
Chapter Five: Résumés – the real scoop	60
Chapter Six: The value of a great letter	75
Chapter Seven: Interviewing	84
Chapter Eight: Negotiating for advantage	102
Chapter Nine: Recruiters – the good, the bad, etc.	119
Chapter Ten: Creating a winning formula	133
Appendix One: Effective versus ineffective	142
Appendix Two: Addressing liabilities	150

Forward

Why you'll want to read this book

This book is written to bring you within range of a desirable job, and help you land one once you get there. If you want a chance at work you enjoy, where you are appreciated for your contributions, and where the pay is better than what you have, you will want to see what this book has to offer.

This is not written with the intent of wasting your time. It is direct and informative, without a lot of distractions. For the sake of brevity, most of the empirical data has been intentionally omitted. Specific examples are in some cases lacking. You don't have time for it, and if I were to write it down it would make this book a lot longer than it needs to be. I don't want to have to write it all down anyway.

Properly applied, this book will uncloak modern myths about job seeking and career changing, help you face the realities, and permit you to understand new paradigms about the job seeking process. If you will read and heed the words that follow, you will improve your chances significantly in the job hunt.

If I have captured your attention, read on.

Chapter One

The game: What job seeking is about

It's not really a game. It just seems like that sometimes. That's because for most people getting a decent job has never been easy. With few exceptions, people put a lot of effort into getting one. Job seeking is an important aspect of life; and getting a good position, holding on to it, providing for yourself and others is for most of us an aspiration we cling to.

Some jobs are easier to get than others. Jobs that are considered less desirable due to working conditions, social stigma or low pay, will always be around. But the good jobs, the ones that pay better, the ones where you are treated better, the ones with advancement potential, are almost invariably harder to get.

In some periods certain types of people can land jobs quite easily. A few years back when everything high tech was cooking, a computer geek often had many jobs to choose from. But as the economy shifted with the beginning of this century, all that changed. Now the programmers, network analysts and others are still in demand, but not like they used to be. The same applies to other types of positions where at one time there was ample opportunity in your field; but as the economy has shifted, some people have to work hard to find what they are looking for.

As this book is being prepared, job hunting seems to be as hard as ever. In fact, indications are that getting the better jobs could be even harder for everyone as time goes by, and for a number of reasons. Therefore, knowing what to do to capture a good job can make a big difference to your future.

In this book I will go into all of this. I will compare getting the right job to the golden quest – seeking the holy grail, if you will, or awakening the Sleeping Beauty. But at the risk of mixing allegories, I would like to first talk about salmon fishing and bug hunting. Are you with me?

I used to live in Alaska. A lot of people who live in Alaska like to go salmon fishing. In fact people fly in from all parts of the world to tap into some of the best fishing experiences imaginable. Some of them actually catch fish. Others do not.

Is there a shortage of salmon in Alaska? No, not really. Even though there is sometimes a shortage of certain types of salmon in some traditional salmon fishing areas, overall there are lots of salmon in Alaska and there will be for a long time to come. But to catch one you have to go where they are, when they are running up designated streams, and fish intelligently.

Getting the right job can be like salmon fishing. For the most part there are adequate jobs out there. But getting to the right place at the right time, with the right equipment, and the right know how in order to land a desirable job is a process that challenges most people.

Some people believe that getting a good job is related to how good the economy is. To a degree that is certainly true. Naturally depressed economic times can make job seeking a lot more difficult. Yet even in bad economic times there are jobs available, and people are getting them.

My father-in-law, who is an able businessman, had to leave a good job once. At the time the US economy was rather sluggish. He was asked what he would do, how would he make a living? He responded, "There's still plenty of money to be made out there." And he was right! There was indeed money to be made, and he went out and made some. For the resourceful and skilled there are always opportunities out there, and in many cases it's just a matter of ferreting them out.

This is generally true with job seeking. Even during the Great Depression, more people had jobs than did not, and some people had very good jobs. Though finding a good job is certainly affected by the condition of the economy, that task only becomes more difficult when the economy is down, it is never impossible. Landing the job you want in many cases is mostly a matter of leveraging the right opportunities. If that does not apply to one's case, then it is a matter of one being flexible enough to secure the work that is out there.

You may not believe what I just said. And perhaps it is not always the case. But by and large it is the absolute truth. You need to be able to leverage the right opportunity, or adjust your thinking to get what is available. The principle here, simply put, is that people who are either well connected, or who understand what job seeking is truly all about, can usually land a decent job. I am going to demonstrate this in subsequent pages.

When I was a boy we lived on a remote ranch in the back woods of northern California. There was no TV at the time, so for recreation we would often go down to the river. It was actually a creek that ran through our property. On a warm day, while our parents would swim or wade, my brother and I entertained ourselves by exploring for bugs.

Along the bank of the creek were thousands of nice round river stones. (These stones are the type high end landscapers can sell you today for a pretty penny.) Using the right type of stick you could turn a rock over and check for bugs. Some stones had several bugs beneath them, others had none. Sometimes we found the type we were looking for. Frequently we did not. But we never could be sure what type of bug we would find beneath a given stone until we turned one over and looked.

For those who have true ambition, job seeking can be a lot like salmon fishing. But for almost everyone else job seeking is mostly like bug hunting. In salmon fishing you are after a prize. In bug hunting, well, you just want a good bug.

When fishing for salmon you can fish very precisely, with the right bait or lures, in the right stream, the correct river, the right time of day, using the correct techniques, and still catch nothing. For example, if you arrive at the stream on the wrong day of the year, there will be no salmon in the river. Either they already swam upstream, or they haven't arrived where you are yet. Salmon are seasonal, and only hit certain streams on certain days of the year. If you are there on the wrong day there are no fish, so you will catch none.

But supposing you do get there during the salmon run, chances are there will be a lot of people there at the same time trying to catch them. Assuming you are in Alaska, bears also show up and sometimes compete with their human counterparts for the best spots along the river. Sometimes the salmon are extremely plentiful, and catching them would seem easy, but if you employ the wrong techniques to catch them you will still come away from the stream empty, despite their plenitude.

I have known of people who have flown to Alaska all the way from Europe to catch a few salmon, only to go away empty because they did not understand the timing or the techniques to catch the fish they wanted. Unfortunately, something like this happens every day in job seeking. People arrive in the job market with a limited understanding of what the business of job seeking is all about and go away empty.

Bug hunting is a bit more straightforward than salmon fishing. You go to the river on the day you want and start flipping over river stones. You keep turning them over with sticks until you find the right bug. When the river is high you won't get many bugs. If you come after a lot of rain, the bugs may have been washed away. If you don't have the right stick you won't be able to flip over the rocks. Or if you do not know what part of the river to go bug hunting at you won't harvest very many.

But bug hunting is easier than salmon fishing, and less expensive. If you pursue your craft with diligence and persistence you will eventually turn over the right rock, find the right bug, and if you have a jar to put him in, you go away happy. And that's the way a lot of people look for jobs. With salmon fishing, well, it is usually a lot harder.

If you are going to go after a top job you need to know what you are doing. You need to understand the rules of the game. If you are willing to settle for a bug in a jar, then you don't need to read this book any further, just get yourself a stick and go look for a good place with a lot of rocks.

But if you want to catch a few beautiful, silvery salmon, take pictures of yourself with your prize, smoke it to delectable morsels, and engorge yourself during the holidays on the kind of fish everyone wants -- while getting to show your pictures to your friends of you by the river holding a string of trophy fish -- then you will need to play the game smartly. So it is with job seeking.

Chapter Two

Good jobs, bad jobs

A few pages ago we talked about the desire of people to land a good job, and we identified some of the things that constitute a good job. Essentially, a good job is where you are treated well, and adequately compensated for your contributions.

As you look around you discover some people have good jobs, others don't. What's the difference in who gets the good ones and who doesn't? Naturally people with a good career track tend to get better jobs. But some don't. Those with a college degree well matched to the requirements of a given industry usually do well. But not always. In fact credible credentials, applicable intelligence, education, and experience, although helpful to landing a good job, are no assurance you are going to get one.

What's the difference then between those who get good jobs and those who don't? People get good jobs because they know how to identify good opportunities and sell themselves effectively. Typically, the person who knows how to find out where "the action" is, then truly sell himself effectually, will always be a leg up on someone who does not.

You can identify people with identical credentials and background and ask, who will land the good job? The answer is, the one who can size up the situation accurately, then present himself more effectively to a prospective employer. Everyone else will settle for what's left.

As we get further into this, we will talk about how to sell yourself effectively. But first I would like to talk about how people who waste time and energy in a job search, then end up with a "not so good" job. Once you understand what not to do, we can devote more space to the business of doing it right.

Finding a job you don't want really isn't a matter of intentionally going out and trying to find a bad job. No one really does that consciously. It is simply a matter of going to find a job in ways that eat up too much time and energy, which obliges you to eventually settle for what is likely to be a bad job.

Since no one starts out trying to get a bad job, how is it that so many people end up with one anyway? The answer is simple. They follow the crowd. In today's world how do people traditionally look for jobs? That's a simple one. They look in the newspaper or on an electronic job board for job listings and begin to apply for the jobs they believe they are qualified for.

Traditionally responding to newspaper ads has been the most common form of job seeking. The modern approach is using Internet job boards to identify openings. You know which ones I mean... Monster, Indeed.com, Career Builder, etc. Unfortunately for most people, responding to listed openings is perhaps the least effective of all traditional approaches.

In an article on job board effectiveness from a few years ago a survey was taken of employers who use job boards for recruiting. They found that only between one and three percent of the job listings on job boards are actually filled from on-line applicants. Yes, you heard right.

How can that be? Only two percent of the jobs posted get filled from on-line applicants? That's right! And taking into consideration the thousands of people who every day apply to these postings the chances of you landing a position from one of these board listings is at least one in 5,000. (This assumes only 100 applicants per opening and sometimes there are up to

1,000, so in such case you could be talking odds of up to 50,000 to one.) For most of us that means our chances of winning the lottery, being blown up by a terrorist, or being gunned down in a movie theater are about the same as getting a job from an Internet listing. Hopefully this is not always the case.

Though more and more people today are using the Internet to find jobs, and with this methodology you can identify thousands of jobs, even though you can drill down on various opportunities on the web, for the most part few of these so called openings are actually waiting for the right applicant. That's because those who list the good jobs are typically filling their positions from other sources, or not filling them at all.

This does not mean you should not apply to jobs on the Internet, because if you have your résumé loaded you can often apply to a position with the click of a mouse. But if your expectation is to surface a lot of opportunities this way you will likely be disappointed. It is all right to do it, just that it is not a very effective activity, and there is only a low probability you will be able to land one that way. So you should avoid concentrating your efforts on doing this, because job hunting based on listed jobs is both inefficient, and only marginally productive.

Some people do get jobs from checking listings online or even looking in the newspaper. (This is probably because this is where they spend most of their time during their search.) However, applying for listed jobs is not normally an effective use of your time because typically hundreds of applications are processed before any real hiring takes place. The odds are against you in this endeavor because the hiring system for most companies is basically against you.

Related to this, one thing you should not do is waste time filling out job applications. You see, an application is designed by a given company to make it easier to screen applicants, which means the application is designed to keep you from getting a job. So if the company does not have a real job for which you are well qualified, you should not waste your time completing applications. (Sometimes a receptionist will hand you an application merely to get rid of you.)

Completing applications to get a job opportunity is generally a waste of time. So you should almost always wait to fill out the application after you have had an interview. By then your chances are greatly enhanced of actually landing the job, and you will be expending your time more productively.

To give you an idea of what is going on here I need to explain something to you about how people are generally hired these days. To orient you I will summarize the candidate screening process used by most companies today, world wide.

Perhaps you, like many people, feel that the most qualified person who has applied for a position is usually the one selected for the job. In reality, beyond minimum qualifications for a given position, the most qualified applicant is frequently eliminated before getting considered. Likewise maybe you feel the person hired from among those who are generally qualified is the one best able to do the job, or will be the most effective. In reality, the most effective person, or the one likely to make the most impact, is often one of the people dropped out of the list when the screening process takes place. Yes, best qualified are sometimes the first to be dropped from consideration!

To understand why this is, you have to understand how companies hire people, and why they do it that way. Let's start with the guy in the company who has an opening he wants to fill.

The fellow will tell someone in the Human Resources Department about the opening and then be asked for a job description of the position needed to be filled. The one trying to hire someone then either pulls a description from the file or writes one himself. The description is then forwarded to HR. Specific requirements for the position are then pulled from the file or drafted up relative to the job description. The HR recruiter then prepares an ad referencing position requirements and the description, and the ad will either run on the Internet or in a newspaper or trade magazine. (Sometimes they will contract a recruiter to help them find the right person.)

As the ads appear, respondents to the ad will send résumés to HR for consideration, and they will pull what appear to be qualified applicants from the results of the postings. Sometimes company representatives will use word searches from electronically saved résumés to help select a group of applicants.

From here someone in HR is then assigned as a screener. This person is rarely a decision maker but most often a clerical worker. To guide him or her, the worker is provided with a checklist outlining the desired skills for the position. In the meantime, HR representatives and others in the company set about advising people they know about the position, and the person trying to fill it may (if he has not already done so) look at the subordinates he currently has in his organization to see if he can identify someone internally.

Within about three weeks after the ad is run in the newspaper, or a few days after it has been listed on the web, the screener will sift through the résumés received (or ones provided by the recruiter) and assign them a priority according to the qualifications checklist she or he is using. Some résumés go into the well-qualified stack, others go into a "maybe" stack, and others are relegated to oblivion.

Most of the time the screener is spending from three to eight seconds to review each résumé. About 80% of the résumés under consideration flunk this screening and are eliminated.

The supervisor for the person doing the screening, or another screener, then goes through the stack of qualified résumés and reassigns them into the good stack or the not so good one. In this process some candidates who may have seemed well qualified at first are assigned to the second stack for any reason under the sun. Once in a while the one who the screener did not feel was all that qualified gets put into the first stack because of perceived special talent, skills or education.

In this pass the second screener may devote up to 20 or 30 seconds to each résumé. But again about 80% of those he or she started with are systematically eliminated.

The "well-qualified" stack, now significantly depleted, is then sifted once more to select candidates for a screening interview with HR, and a call is made to schedule this initial interview. Some of these can't be reached or are already working. The remainder are screened again over the phone based upon a few screening questions the caller has put together to ask the applicant. Usually 80% of those spoken to on the phone are screened out. Those few who survive this screening are asked in for the in-person interview.

Here are some of the reasons people get screened out:

1. Too much experience. Most companies don't want someone who is either too old, or will draw too high a pay, or who may be "too smart" for everybody else.

2. Not enough experience. Most companies do not want to go through the agony of having to spend a lot of effort training someone. They need a certain amount of experience to do the job, or a specific set of skills, education and background, or both. For guidance on what experience is needed they go back to the job description drafted by the one wanting to hire someone.

3. Wrong type of experience. If the person is considered not a good match according to what was written in the first place, then good bye.

4. Looks too expensive. Experience aside, some people portray in their credentials that they make a lot of money. Companies only have so much budgeted for the position in question. If your résumé

comes across as too strong, they probably won't interview you.

5. Not mainstream. If the résumé portrays you as a little out of character for the industry or their company culture, nothing doing.

6. Looks controversial. You may have a background that raises questions or concerns from the screener, whether or not the concerns are justified. If your résumé sounds too good to be true, especially if the claims are unsubstantiated, you could be out of there, rather than in there, in a flash.

7. Liabilities. If it looks like your career progression has holes in it, or if your job history doesn't look smooth, you will probably be eliminated. No sense taking a risk with someone with a weak job history.

8. Wrong background. If you worked for the wrong company or have an unusual background you may get eliminated. Companies pride themselves on doing things a certain way. If you are accustomed to doing them a different way you may be considered a poor culture fit for the folks doing the hiring.

9. Wrong location. If you are not living in the general locale of the position, you may not be seriously considered. The hiring managers will

always look first for people in their local area.

10. Military background. Most companies are afraid of prior military people because they feel the applicant may be set in his ways and hard to deal with. After all, no one wants Gomer Pyle or Sergeant Striker to be part of the organization. They would simply not fit the company culture. Plus few people in the recruiting business have a real appreciation for what military experience is all about. So unless there is some good, recent industry experience the military guy is sent packing.

11. Poorly expressed résumé. You may have a good résumé, but it may not address the requirements of that job or what that company perceives as their real requirements. Or you may have a résumé that does not present your assets very effectively. In either case you will be screened out, even if you are relatively well qualified for the job.

12. Age. If you appear to be too old or too young for what they want to see you will likely be dropped. (Yes, I know this is discriminatory, but they do it all the time.)

13. Poor handling of the phone screening interview. The screening over the phone is a real interview, but since it is over the phone many people are not ready for it. They do not know how to

present themselves well over the phone, or they have not prepared themselves for the questions being asked. Or perhaps they are not as well qualified as they thought, and get separated out by the screening questions.

14. Some other hair-brained reason. Sometimes people are screened out for no reason at all, merely to make the candidate list short and usable. If they have too many applicants, some will be dropped just to make the list more manageable. There could be other unknown reasons for this as well.

An HR person, or recruiter, normally conducts the initial interview. Typically an HR person is an administrator who works HR issues. Many people in this specialty tend to be task oriented and resistant to change. If this is the case it is unlikely anyone will get by them who is too accustomed to thinking for themselves, or desirous of bringing about positive change in the organization.

The questions they ask will normally be canned. Every candidate will be asked the same ones. The interviewer will take notes of his or her impressions. Those who are most impressive will normally be those who can express themselves well and show similar personality characteristics to the one doing the interviewing. A more experienced interviewee will tend to do a bit better. Some research done on the company will usually impress the interviewer. But too much research, or too much of anything else, may scare them off.

Following the screening interviews of everyone available, the written results of the interviews will be forwarded to the HR manager or supervisor who initiated the action some days or weeks before. At this point the superior will take another cut, and the people who do not sound good are screened out and flushed away.

The survivors of the initial interview process will then be screened one more time based on a second interview. This will either be with a senior member of the HR team, or someone who works in the office of the person who wants to fill the position, or perhaps both will conduct a joint interview, or each will interview the remaining candidates individually. Once again canned questions will be the order of the day, and scores will be awarded based on the same issues of concern raised in the résumé phase of the process. Other concerns may surface based on the personality match of the candidates with the interviewer.

For the average position to be filled, few candidates have survived the process so far. But we aren't done yet. Now the hiring authority will get the remainder of the interview documentation and résumés. The HR people will have been very efficient and will send to the hiring manager a list of from two to seven candidates. This manager, presumably the one who wanted to fill the position in the first place, will then make some additional decisions.

First, is there still a need to fill this position? By now several weeks may have past since the initial decision was made. But situations are sometimes fluid. At this point they may decide to not fill the position after all, for a variety of reasons.

Second, perhaps the company leadership will not allow anyone to be hired. Sometimes there are funding restrictions or a hiring freeze in place. Sometimes the big boss merely wants to throw his weight around. In any case, someone up the ladder may decide to nix the hire, and its over!

Third, it's possible that in the meantime the hiring manager has identified another candidate on his own. This could be a friend, relative of someone within the company, or someone specifically recommended by someone he knows. This someone could have referred a good candidate. Or maybe someone he already knows is qualified for the position.

A referred candidate is usually considered a good one because the company has a first hand recommendation from someone within the company or who is known by the company to be reliable, and the candidate already has an entry to the inside. In some cases the person that is eventually hired is already working for the company, and is promoted into the position. Internal advancement is usually considered a good idea, and poof, the position is filled.

Fourth, the requirements for the job may have changed. Perhaps they don't need the guy who can count apples anymore. Now they need someone who can count pears. After all, you can't have too many apple counters hanging around. Or perhaps the job description used to determine who they wanted to hire in the first place has been determined to be out of date or invalid. Oh well. Too bad for all those who applied for that job!

But if none of that happens, the final list of candidates is gone over one more time and the hiring manager discards anyone he does not want to interview. In some cases he has formed initial impressions about the certain candidates from HR or from reviewing the résumés forwarded to him.

So he interviews three, or maybe four, then picks the one he likes best. This could be based on special qualifications the candidate brings to bear, but is most often a factor of personality and compatibility with the interviewer.

You can see that this process is a "last man standing" game. That is, at each stage in the process people are eliminated. It is not always the person who impresses the most that is retained for the next battery of elimination activity, but it is the person that is less objectionable than the rest. This does not mean the most qualified is hired, but the least objectionable is most likely to be given the nod.

Assuming there is a minimum of one candidate left, someone in the organization will tender an offer to the last person remaining. Sometimes the person extending the offer is someone senior to the hiring manager, like the Chief Financial Officer. It is frequently the Human Resources Manager. If the offer is agreeable, and the favored candidate hasn't already taken a position somewhere else, a hire may be consummated. But sometimes not, for a variety of other reasons. Whew!

By this point the process may have taken two to three months. The person hired won't see a paycheck for up to six weeks yet and is sometimes facing some difficulty financially. Even if this is not the case, the hiree may become disillusioned about his or her new job, or after the person starts the boss becomes unhappy with the new person's performance, the new hire is turned loose, and so the process may start all over again.

Realizing that some hires don't take, companies will sometimes over hire. That is, they will take on more people than they intend to keep on the chance someone doesn't work out. That way they have a back up, so they can let someone go, or permit them to leave on their own later.

Now that you have considered a modern hiring process, you can see why applying for a listed job is so haphazard. Even if you are well qualified for a listed position, chances are you won't make the cut somewhere along the line. It's a long shot; the odds are against you. That résumé you send in good faith will most often be used to simply eliminate you. If you are fortunate enough to get an interview, in most cases you are still a long way from landing a job.

As pointed out earlier, some types of jobs are easier to get, and if you have special skills or qualifications you may not need to worry very much. Even if you are seeking a job in an ineffective way you may still pick up a decent position. The rest of us, though, have good reason to want to pursue the most efficient avenues for finding a decent job because the likelihood of failure is too high.

You may ask yourself, if the hiring process is so convoluted and intricate, why do company's prefer to use it?

Three reasons. First they want to avoid a bad hire. A "bad hire" is when you put someone on board who can't do the job, or has a poor work ethic, or a series of vices no one wants to mess with. A bad hire is when you end up with a liability instead of an asset working for you.

So does the HR screening process preclude the acquisition of a bad hire? Not really. It just keeps most people from getting a job with that company. As noted, the process is somewhat inefficient and frequently only those who understand the game will survive it. If a guy is in truth incapable of doing the job the HR process may weed him out somewhere along the line.

But someone who is slick, persuasive or who has lied on his résumé, or someone who has a minor personality disorder, may still get in, and then the company has to deal with it. It's often unpleasant and expensive to do so, but that's the way the system works in today's world.

A second reason companies employ less efficient methods of hiring people is bad management. This means either the hiring authority does not really know what he wants, does not understand his real needs, or he communicates it poorly to HR or the recruiter. Perhaps the company is employing ineffective recruiting tactics, and starts out with a poor list of candidates to begin with. Or maybe the boss wants someone working for him who thinks like him, regardless of his or her qualifications.

Another reason good people often don't get hired is what is perceived as a potential liability to the company. Some people may be assessed as having a potential personal problem, and to avoid the possibility that something could go wrong, the company takes precautions, and hiring does not take place.

There are many people in special categories these days who are empowered because of special rights. This includes people with disabilities, minorities, or even females – those who may be disposed to hire a lawyer and come after companies who discriminate, or that give the impression of discriminating against people in protected classes.

In some cases (usually for federal contractors) military veterans enjoy special hiring privileges. Therefore it's important for people who are doing the hiring to understand all the potential liabilities associated with the hiring process, and to know what to ask and not to ask when interviewing and screening people.

The HR folks are the logical ones to understand these things and are often hired specifically because of that understanding. They supposedly are trained to know how to avoid tort liability when managing the hiring process and that's why they work in HR.

Most companies are not equipped to change the hiring process because the hiring manager is often too busy doing his job to spool through 200 résumés to pick someone he wants. He lets HR do all the stubby pencil work before he gets involved because it's easier on him. By the same token, an HR person is frequently over burdened with a variety of issues to waste too much time on the screening process.

As we have shown, the traditional hiring process is fraught with inefficiencies for the company. Frequently people with great talent and ability are eliminated early in the process. Other times interviewers reject talented people for questionable reasons. That is, they screen people out that may look like they pose a liability if hired, when in reality there's nothing wrong with the candidate at all. While at the same time too often people who are marginally qualified or a bit dishonest slip through the screen and land jobs they don't truly deserve.

It's a tragedy of modern business. The hiring process is poised to weed out undesirables, but in their zeal to do so, the ones doing the screening end up weeding out some of the best candidates, and most talented people. As sad as that is, for those who are trying to get a decent job, it's a reality we all just have to deal with.

So where does that leave you, the job seeker? Spinning your wheels week after week, applying for jobs and getting turned away. Finally, in desperation, you will do like many do: settle for a job you don't want. You put the bug in a jar and go home with it.

So, is there a solution? You bet there is. Is it an easy one? Hey, in this world nothing of true value is very easy. But for the resourceful and persistent job seeker there is a light down there in the darkness.

Chapter Three

Assaulting the fairy castle

As everyone knows, there is a secret list of jobs that are unpublished anywhere else, and if you can pay the purveyor of this secret list enough money you will get the job you want. Right?

No, there is no secret list of unpublished jobs. But you may have heard of the famous "Unpublished Job Market" that a lot of folks are dying to tell you about. It is true there are actually a great deal of positions that are filled every day without ever being published or listed. In fact some have said that as many as 80% to 90% of all positions are filled before they are ever officially listed with anyone.

Frankly, I cannot say if this is correct. If indeed these positions are never published, it is significantly difficult to come to an accurate assessment of how many positions are actually filled this way. But the concept is right on. Many, many positions are filled every day without any formal listing of the job or position.

Naturally, since these positions are not listed with anyone, there can be no secret list of the openings. You might know someone for whom this is a difficult concept. If so, have them think about it for a moment… no openings listed, no list of openings. Capisci?

It is true you can find special listings for certain positions in trade journals or specialty publications that have limited circulation. Sometimes there are fewer applicants for these positions. There are also Internet sites where you pay a subscription fee to access, and where there are special job postings with limited exposure. Even so you are still responding to openings, the percent return on these is still ridiculous, and for the most part you are using your time ineffectively.

So what is it about the real, so called "hidden job market"? How does one find out about the jobs being brokered every day? And how do you get yourself in a position to take advantage of them?

In many cases, as I mentioned before, the job finds the person, not the other way around. I've known many people who, in the bulk of their careers, never had to look for a position, because the position always found them. They would get a call from someone they knew and this person would ask if they were interested in such and such a position. If so there would be a discussion and the person called would soon have a new job. The job they got was never listed but they were hired into a desirable position anyway. Thus the value of being well respected in your field.

In other cases people work for the same organization most of their lives and don't worry about getting a job. They may live a boring life, and may put up with a lot of grief on the job over the years, but they stick it out to a point where job seeking never enters the picture. But this is typically Hollywood stuff. Most people end up changing jobs several times throughout their career and have to suffer through the process.

Before I give you the answer to address this dilemma of trying to find unlisted jobs, I would like to discuss the allegory of Sleeping Beauty's Castle. (Yeah, okay, but this won't be too long.)

In the Sleeping Beauty story the princess falls asleep inside a walled castle due to an evil spell. The only one who can wake her is a handsome prince. When the spell is cast, thorny vines grow up all over the outside of the castle and it is virtually hidden from view.

The prince learns about the sleeping princess and desires to wake her. But first he must slay the dragon. Employing great valiance he faces the evil dragon and casts his sword into the creature's heart. He then approaches the castle, negotiates the moat and hacks away at the vines until he can access the walls. There he is faced with walls that are a hundred feet high and 60 feet thick. He can't get in.

In the fairy tale some magic happens and he makes it into the castle, searches everywhere until he finds the princess, kisses her, and she wakes. The two then ride off in romantic bliss. The story bears a resemblance to the eternal quest of finding the fabled holy grail. The gifted knight goes from land to land, from city to city, from rumored location to speculated location, in a perpetual quest for the wondrous grail.

Though the story is apparently mythological, even myth does not specify exactly what the holy grail actually is (or was.) For some it is the cup or chalice from which Christ drank at the Last Supper. For others it is a receptacle that captured some of Christ's blood that was shed while he was on the cross. Some also believe that the holy grail was actually a woman, supposedly Mary Magdalene.

For the purposes of our story it is not important what the fabled object actually was. We will let others try to sort it all out. But for the sake of our allegory, let us pretend the fabled holy grail was actually a woman. Let us pretend that what you are seeking is the ravishing "Sleeping Beauty" of fairy tales.

In your case, you are the prince trying to get into the castle to rescue your true love. In our story the castle represents a company where a job can be located. In assaulting this castle let's say you put a lot of effort into getting inside, and go through all the gyrations, but in your case there is no magic, no fairy tale ending, just a lot of hard work. That's because you are not employing all the assets at your disposal.

Metaphorically, here is what you are obliged to do: First you have to slay the dragon. This dragon is hateful and destructive and threatens to devour you. The dragon represents the destructive influences of frustration, hopelessness and despair, the common lot of almost all job seekers. But you step forward with armor and sword and defeat this monster through your positive attitude and conscientious application of good job seeking principles. Whew, what a task!

Then you must negotiate the moat or swamp. This represents all the misinformation out there about job seeking. This you overcome by referring to appropriate sources (like this book) for information about accomplishing the task, and ignore the naysayers who have no idea what they are talking about. To do this you must enter the moat and hang on to your horse as he swims through the filthy stream and brings you safely across.

The horse represents the Real Truth about job seeking. With his strength you can penetrate the void of half truths and misinformation you are confronted with. He is the powerful steed that will get you past obstacles and thrust you into action, stands by you and holds you up during perilous and grievous battles, thus permitting you to eventually come off the victor.

Next you have the thorny vines. These you hack through with your sword while protecting yourself from the thorns with your shield. The vines represent the resistance inherent in job seeking coming from all those who are competing with you, or who interfere in your endeavor. With persistence you vanquish this obstacle as well.

Finally, exhausted, you reach the walls of the castle. You now discover they are high, strong and impenetrable. The walls represent the natural barriers every company has to people getting into their company. These walls are constructed to keep invaders out, and are set up so that only certain people can be let in. Companies establish these boundaries to help them feel that they are hiring only the best qualified people, or only those who meet the criteria someone has established to permit a hire to occur.

On the walls, to insure you are kept out, there are people with long pikes, spears and bows and arrows to provide seemingly unconquerable resistance. These are the Human Resources people, the gatekeepers such as secretaries, receptionists and others whose mission it is to screen you out, and insure you do not get in, all with the purpose of making you give up and go elsewhere.

You are also faced with the daunting task of trying to scale the wall wearing full armor, while the people on the wall are there continually pushing you down, and trying to skewer you with pikes, spears and arrows. "This is not working," you conclude. "I need someone on the inside to let me in."

Fortunately you have a few arrows. You can lob these over the wall and hope they land somewhere. The arrows represent your résumé. But you have no way of knowing where the arrow is landing, or if anyone will ever actually read your résumé. Certainly the HR people are not doing this. In fact they are quite busy shredding the résumé of every poor soul who is trying to get in.

Ill-informed people who do not understand the basic concepts of successful job seeking assume a recruiter on the inside is going to snatch their résumé from one of those arrows being fired over the wall and instantly invite them into the castle for a glass of wine. But please bear in mind, typically the recruiter is inside drinking wine with the king, if he is in there at all. In any case he is likely disinterested in your plight.

You can see the evil fairy, or queen of darkness, who has created all these obstacles has done a good job of blocking your success. But fortunately you are courageous, and your trusted steed is undaunted. You forge ahead, your helmeted head unbowed.

This is where you turn to your key contacts, trusted friends and acquaintances to identify someone who lives on the inside of the castle, has not been placed under the spell of the evil fairy, and who can lower the drawbridge to let you in. You have a secret confidant on the inside who has access to keys that can open doors. It takes some effort for you to establish contact with the right person, and to induce him to help you, but eventually you find this special person, and are ushered into the great fortress, with only a bit of fanfare.

Once this happens you can work the inside of the castle, going from place to place until you find the sleeping princess. This princess of course represents the job you are after, the holy grail, if you will. In time, and after considerable effort, you finally locate her. You kiss her gently, she awakes from her magical sleep and embraces you. You sweep her into your arms and happily follow her into wedded bliss.

In regards to the allegory, as is implied, once you get inside the castle there is still plenty of work to do to find the princess and get access to the chamber where she is in repose. But once you are over the walls the hard part is usually over. Given enough time and a little resourcefulness you can normally find that true Sleeping Beauty and take her home. The full application of this allegory is the key to successful job seeking.

I hope you are paying attention to the above process. Successful job seeking does not depend so much on what you know, but usually depends more upon who you know. It is not necessarily a process of proving your qualifications, although that is part of the equation, but more than that, it is an exercise in approaching the right people in the right way to come away victorious. This may be a surprise to some, but not to others.

Now some people are going to say I am talking about "networking" here. You know, networking -- that is where you cash in your friends and relatives until someone caves in and finds a job for you. No I am not talking about "classic" networking. I am talking about People-Charging your campaign.

People-Charging. That's what you do. You charge your campaign with the right people, and give it power through these people. You get them involved in your campaign, and follow their lead to victory.

"People-charging" is different than networking in the classic sense. It is a method of networking to be sure, but it does not involve cashiering your friends and contacts for your selfish ends. It is a matter of involving others in your campaign without them feeling they are imposed upon, and in such a way that they are happy to help you, and become interested in your campaign's success.

If you do this right, job seeking can be a lot easier than you think, and can provide positive results, with lasting friendships and contacts remaining intact. It is also a method that provides you with the contacts you need to be successful. It places you in direct contact with the person who can lower the drawbridge and help you find the sleeping princess.

Insofar as job seeking goes, people-charging your campaign is the secret to success. It is the way to find the good jobs rather than the bad. It is what permits you to claim the beautiful princess that may very well have been sleeping on your own front porch all this time. And it is what gives you access to the before mentioned "hidden job market."

Chapter Four

How to people charge your campaign

How to be successful in the endeavor of working with others is not too complicated once you have learned a few basic principles. You start from the known and move to the unknown. What does this mean?

To understand it let's examine how to identify your family tree. (This is applicable to the discussion, believe me.) Let's also say for the sake of argument that you are related to Paul Revere. You want to know how you are related to him so you can demonstrate it to your family and others, and perhaps pass the legacy of your noteworthy ancestor to your children.

In an effort to identify your relationship to Mr. Revere you go back to old records and histories and, after careful research, identify all of Paul Revere's children. He had several. You discover the man's first wife died after having a number of children, then he had a large second family by his second wife. But you are not dissuaded, and carefully chronicle all of the man's many offspring. Then you take it a step further and identify his grandchildren, then the great grandchildren and so forth.

After about five generations of this you have many, many people on your list. In fact with a man as prolific as Mr. Revere, you will likely have several thousand by this time. And what is tragic about it is that you still do not know who you are related to. I mean, among all of these descendants of the great Paul Revere, you have not yet matched your genealogy with his. This is depressing.

But let's say you do it the other way. Instead of starting with records from early in Boston, you start with records of your own immediately family. Your grandparents have told someone in the past who it is that has traced the family tree. You check with living relatives and soon you have a rather extensive list of your own, known relatives. From here you can pursue a line, generation by generation backwards, until you link up with a known history of Mr. Revere's kin.

You have succeeded. You now know how you are related. And you have an accurate record of everyone of note in your particular line also, with limited guesswork, and a lot less wasted time. You may not know the names of all of Mr. Revere's descendants, but you know the ones you are most closely related to. That was your objective in the first place.

How does this apply to looking for a job? Well, like checking the family tree, it's a whole lot easier if you <u>work from the known to the unknown</u>. You have more control of the outcome and you will waste a lot less time.

Why is this? Because you are starting with people who know you and are much more willing to work with you. You won't have to labor for days trying to get in to see them. They are people you already have a relationship with and who will normally be happy to meet with you.

From them you are in a position to meet and work with people who know the people your associates know, and you are better able to make a connection. Ask the people you know for information on other people and ask for permission to use that friend's name in contacting them. Not too difficult, right?

While you are doing this you can prepare yourself to make soft contacts elsewhere. A soft contact is someone you may not know real well, but will nevertheless be comparatively easy to get in to see. Who are these types of people? Well there are a surprising number of them you can go to.

First you can speak with association leaders. Associations are organizations dealing with a given industry or interest. The value of approaching associations is that it is relatively easy to get in to see representatives of these organizations, and usually they can point you to contacts they have in given companies. They will often be the best soft source for reaching out to those who are influential in their industry. They could include business or professional associations, or economic development organizations.

Associations could also include clubs and service organizations, as well as chambers of commerce. Any of them can provide you introductions to people who are well connected in business or the community. If you belong to the same volunteer organization as someone else you also probably have a good in.

Alumni are an excellent source of people to speak with. Most people who went to the same college as you will be willing to meet with you due to your similar backgrounds. Some of these alumni are probably serving in leadership positions of various companies and may be able to help significantly.

Political leaders are often people who know a lot of people. Elected local representatives are invariably well connected and will tend to know everyone in town. Those who work on campaigns or who belong to political organizations are equally well connected. No political organization can survive for long without donations and these people know who the donors are. Most political leaders will meet readily with a new person, especially one who is spouting party rhetoric.

Religious leaders are not all that different from politicians. They usually make their living by knowing people and working with people throughout a community. It does not matter what religion you are, you will find meeting religious leaders fertile ground to plow in. You will soon be able to meet well connected people in their congregation, key donors, business leaders, community activists, volunteers and the like.

You do not have to be religious to work with religious leaders. Bear in mind that many of them are not very religious themselves. But they enjoy the role and are invariably well connected to people in the community.

Other community leaders will also likely be willing to meet with you. If you live in a given city or town, or are contemplating moving into a certain area, you will be able to meet people involved in a variety of endeavors who are happy to know you. These can include neighborhood associations, public service organizations, charities, school district volunteers, parent or school organizations, youth sporting associations, veterans organizations and many like entities. Leaders of these organizations will know people. You should include them on your list. Your list could also include anyone who is active in the community. People who work with charities, or are trying to secure donors for a worthy cause are typically well connected and should be approached.

These are your soft contacts.

You should now develop lists of people you know, as well as the soft contacts, such as fellow alumni, and people in organizations who will most likely be willing to meet with you. Naturally, starting with those organizations connected to business or economics would tend to make the most sense. But which type organization you go after in the long run is not as important. The point is you should work the soft contacts before trying direct contact with companies, with the strategy of asking the former to introduce you to other people you want to meet, or asking for their assistance in identifying people you need to meet.

As you meet with them you should explain what you are after and why you are meeting with them, <u>clarifying to them you are not asking them to get you a job</u>, merely to give you advice and information. As long as you focus on getting information and introductions you will not turn people away, they will normally be glad to help you, and you will get better assistance from them than you would if you were asking about a job.

Let me repeat that. Until you are actually in a job interview, never, ever, ever ask for a job, opening, opportunity or position! Let me say that again: when networking, NEVER ASK FOR A JOB! Just ask for information, and advice, then ask them who you should be talking with. Don't use the term "opportunity," "opening" or "position." Tell them you are seeking advice, information and maybe some intelligence, but not a job. You are not expecting this of them. Should you ask about a specific job the answer will be "we have no openings" and your interview with them will be at an end. However, if you focus on getting information, the intelligence they provide can be very valuable to you.

Armed with this, you can find out where the true openings are lurking, or possibly induce someone to hire you even though they do not have an official opening. In some cases the information garnered will permit you to be effective in identifying a specific opportunity on your own.

By asking only for advice and information, your contacts will tend to empathize with your situation and will usually be willing to provide the type of assistance you request – advice and information. Most people like to provide advice, and providing information is also something most people will be willing to do. Either of these activities puts them in the position of a mentor. And most people enjoy this role. You have therefore enlisted their assistance in moving your campaign forward. One of these contacts could eventually be the one who gets you into the castle.

When you get a referral from one of your contacts, ask this contact for permission to use his or her name. Do not let them call for you! (They will either forget or not represent you as well as you can yourself.) Tell them thanks, but that you would not want to inconvenience them further. Take down the information, and make the contact yourself.

Where the person you are contacting does not already know you, you should always send a letter to them first, telling them who referred you, and asking to meet with them for a few minutes. Keep your meeting to 15 to 30 minutes, no more. Thank them personally at the conclusion of the meeting. Then send a thank you note later. At a minimum send them a pleasant email thanking them.

If the person cannot meet you at the office, then arrange for breakfast or lunch meetings. If this is a community, religious or political leader you can often meet with them evenings or weekends. If you are trying to meet someone outside your area, either plan a trip to meet with them (combine the trip with meeting others at the same time to conserve your resources) or arrange a telephone discussion. You could also engage in a Skype meeting if your contacts will do so.

To make this exercise effective you must develop information on people you wish to contact. This means identifying business leaders and folks working in specific companies. You also want to develop lists of companies to target. You will need to be able to identify companies by size, industry and situation (whether they are solvent, growing, or shrinking.)

Probably the quickest and fastest way to get the type of information you need is through the Internet. For job seeking, Google is your friend. Schedule some time on the computer to ferret out the names, organizations and people you are interested in approaching. The Internet has an astounding amount of information on almost every subject, including US and international businesses.

Today one of the best sources of contact information is LinkedIn. If you are not already a subscriber you should subscribe immediately, and begin building your electronic network. There are various ways to do this. Try to identify people who are super users and have a lot of contacts already. Then network with them. Or join a series of interest groups and target people in these groups. Once you have a powerful network built up, use it judiciously to approach people you want to meet or want to get to know better.

In addition to LinkedIn you may be able to identify other business networking sites. There are also a number of social networking sites. Though not as good as LinkedIn for networking purposes, they are nevertheless good sources, in most cases, for peoples names and information about their employment.

A reference librarian in a good well-equipped library can also help. One can help you identify lists of companies in your field. Usually a local business journal or other entity publishes a Book of Lists or similar document which identifies regional private and public companies. (Sometimes university libraries have more useful data than other small pubic libraries.) You should also ask the reference librarian for any other business directories for the area. Unfortunately some of these directories cannot be copied because of copy write infringement issues. But sometimes there are independent directories of companies within certain industries that are not restricted.

In addition to the above, there are library lists available via computer or CD these days that can be quite valuable to you. Certain database providers can also provide some very good information to public libraries, much of which can be accessed via computer.

Another place to get lists is through business associations or chambers of commerce. A good career consulting company may be able to provide many lists of companies as part of their consulting fee. Check out the companies capabilities, though, before you sign on the dotted line, so you will know what you can and cannot get from them. The <u>currency</u> of these lists is vital.

For lists of alumni the best place to look is the alumni association of the college in question. You will want to be on good terms with your alumni association to garner their lists. Some alumni lists are better than others, but anything they can provide could be valuable.

Churches normally have directories of key members, as do clubs, associations business organizations and other institutions. If you are politically active you can often gain access to lists of registered voters in your area. But use caution in how you use this information so you do not infringe on privacy laws or other provisions.

Currency and usability of the data is important. Dunn & Bradstreet and other providers often make company information available to libraries. But bear in mind the information they provide on companies, especially smaller companies, may not be particularly current. Prices for obtaining this data may vary.

Some on-line resources can provide information through their site. Sometimes you will need to pay for a subscription to get it. But you can often discover good, current info. But bear in mind that information on small or privately held companies may be totally absent from many commercial lists, because they tend to focus on major corporations. Also, some data does not download easily. It is sometimes delivered in cumbersome script files that make it nearly impossible to manipulate once you have it. It is all right for a handful of companies, but once you start working with longer lists of companies, and various contacts, you have your work cut out for you.

Recruiters and search firms use a variety of sources for finding people. Some of these are very good and they are sometimes available on line for free. I have used some very powerful data sources made available through these providers. But since some of these charge considerable sums to their magic data, it may be too costly for a job seeker to secure information to many of these sources.

Anyway, using the best data available to you, you should identify business leaders in your industry so you can ask your contacts for introductions to them. These are your targets. You should initially ask these leaders of your targeted companies for a meeting to glean information from them. Many will not speak with you even though you are being introduced through one of your contacts. But some will. Use creative strategies to get inside the company to speak with them on a business basis. Provide them with a good business letter and practice your telephone techniques.

Don't let discouragement wear you down. Go after your soft contacts first and let them lead you to the harder contacts until you are inside the castle and talking with the people outside Sleeping Beauty's door.

Chapter Five

Résumés – the real scoop

You can talk with a thousand people and get a thousand different opinions on résumés. Everyone has a perspective on them and each person's perspective tends to be narrow.

A big argument centers around the concept of whether a good résumé should be chronological or functional. Chronological résumés focus on where a person has worked, breaking down the dates a person arrived and departed and what the person did at each station. Functional résumés focus on performance, avoiding the specific dates and other characteristics of the chronological version.

Other opinions about résumés are regularly argued, especially what should be included in the résumé and how long it should be. Some favor a brief résumé, others tout the advantages of a two to three page document. Some insist a résumé be easy to read and well formatted. Others say forget that, just cram it with data. Others speak out in favor of a longer more formal document. Some publish rules on what you can and cannot say. Others are less finicky.

Here's my bent on it: The characteristics of a résumé should be determined by how the document is being used. The layout and content of your résumé should be based on what you're going to use it for. Whether a given résumé is good or bad is sometimes a function of its application more so than its content.

In other words, a document provided to a prospective employer must conform to the context of the contact you are making. If this is a first, initial or original contact then brevity and functionality are the order of the day. But if the person already knows you, or you have already passed through a screening process, then a longer, more traditional format is probably preferred.

To understand these guidelines better, let us return to our earlier discussion of how the hiring system works in the today's world. When a position is first announced, the HR department or company recruiter goes out and solicits or conjures up a large number of résumés by posting ads or using public listings, then reviews them in a rather cursory manner until they have selected a number that pass muster. Then the remaining are reviewed again by someone else, then initial screening interviews are conducted, then a face to face interview occurs. Some situations differ slightly, but this is the general process.

On an initial screening your résumé will enjoy the light of day from between three and 20 seconds on the first pass. If it survives the first pass, it will likely get 20 to 40 seconds on the second pass. The hottest résumés will probably get a three minute review. Then that's it.

If you are still alive at this juncture, then and only then do you get to speak with someone from that company. If your résumé did not hold their interest you are out of there! If you are undergoing an electronic scan, then the scan will take about one to five seconds, and will be done by a computer.

Typically an HR department will gather the résumés to be considered for a certain position and compile them for a visual review. If they have more than a couple of hundred they will lighten the stack artificially until they get a number they can work with. Cover letters are routinely trashed at this point also (not always, but quite often) then the pages of the résumé after the first one are very often discarded. The person doing the screening then has a one page document to go through. This will save them time.

If the screener does not encounter the information he or she is seeking on that one page during the first pass, you will be relegated to oblivion. Too bad! What a nice résumé you had and there it is, in someone's trash bin.

But if the résumé is in the trash instead of on the desk it is your fault, because you did not give the screener what he or she wanted to see on the first page for the trip through the screening process. If we are talking electronic scan, then the computer is looking for key words, terms and buzz words. Those things all need to be in there to be safe.

Today many companies and most recruiters scan résumés into an electronic system and then, when they are seeking someone, they search for résumés based upon key words. If your résumé has the terms or buzz words they have keyed in, then your résumé gets viewed visually. If not, well, too bad.

Once this electronic process is completed, the résumés claimed from the database will get a visual review. Now we are back to where we were before. The résumés that tell their story effectively on the first page make it through the system. Others are systematically, and very rapidly, screened into Never Land.

In cases where you have emailed a résumé to someone as an attachment, very possibly the recipient declined to open the attached file and your electrons are dashed to oblivion. Pasted résumés will sometimes get a look, but what they are looking for has to be obvious from the beginning, otherwise you are out. In addition, résumés pasted into an email seldom look very professional. If the recruiter or screener is interested in opening an attached résumé you may have a chance. But bear in mind, if too much of the important content of that résumé is buried on the second page you are still dead.

Now let's say your résumé gets past the screener and the initial interviewer, and your credentials are presented to the senior HR person or the person who is doing the recruiting. Perhaps from there they go to a decisions maker for a late stage review. What does this person want to see?

In this case you are not getting just a cursory look, but the person reviewing your credentials wants to be able to do some reading, so will look deeper into the document. So what do they want to see at this point? Something specific and to the point, that addresses the requirements of the job, while telling the recipient enough about you so they have a feel for who you are.

If all they have is a one-page document they may feel they do not have enough to properly consider a person.

Therefore, frequently the one-page document you may have initially tendered for consideration here is not the right document for a more in-depth screening. The reader wants to see content not glitz, and your résumé now needs to address these more in-depth requirements.

At this point then you will want to present a two-page, easy to read document so the reviewer can have a better look at you. This then must be a different type of résumé. This is what a decision maker comes to expect, and he or she may be disappointed at only being able to handle a one-page gem that was used in the screening.

Often outside recruiters may express dismay at the "first approach" résumé they have received. The document clearly reflects the person is qualified, but it is not pretty enough to present to the recruiter's client. So a recruiter will sometimes report that the shortened, "first-pass" résumé they possess does not meet standards and that they want to see a different résumé. Some folks interpret this as a sign the résumé they may have been using is faulty. They fail to take into consideration the recruiter's perspective on the situation.

The recruiter at this point is looking for a "presentation résumé" to go forward to the next level.

Recruiters and HR staffers do not call people up to critique résumés. Some of them wade through a few thousand per day. They hardly have time for such antics. No, if they call you it is not because the résumé they have seen so far is faulty, but because it has done its job. The request for a "better" résumé is merely a request for something in a broader format.

In this stage of the process the only thing you as the job seeker need to be concerned about is insuring the recruiter sees whatever he wants to. Give them a résumé with a different look and everyone will be happy: the recruiter, the decision-maker, and you.

Now that you understand the difference between a first pass résumé and a "consideration" or "presentation" résumé, let's talk briefly about what the résumé should include and how it should be formatted. To address this discussion we need to first know what a résumé is. Many people think that a résumé is a compilation of all they are and can be. They tend to build extensive documentation with a lot of extraneous baloney included. Don't fall for this.

In Europe and some other regions of the world you see this tendency born out. They use something called a CV, or curriculum vitae. In the US these things are still used in academic circles to present a professor's credentials. But in the real world of business a CV is not only passé but is also venomous. That is why the résumé concept is becoming more and more prevalent in the world today.

Think about it. What is a résumé? What is it used for? Is it supposed to be a life history? Is that what people want to see when they are reviewing your credentials? Heck no! A résumé is nothing more or less than a sales brochure. That's right, a sales brochure. Its purpose is to create enough interest in you as the product that people will want to talk with you.

The résumé is not a museum piece used to get the job. It is not a life story, or even a chronicle of your complete work history. It is there to sell you to the screener or reviewer and get you the interview, that's all!

If you thought résumés get you a job this may be a shock to you. A résumé does not do that. You get the job from interviewing, not résumé writing. The purpose of the résumé is merely to get you in front of people. Its function is to sell you to the screener so you get to talk to the people making the decisions.

Now let's talk about the principal function of a résumé from the employer's standpoint. Once someone sees your résumé, what is the résumé typically used for? If you go back to our earlier discussion on "the last man standing concept" you will note that the résumé is principally used by the company to eliminate you.

If this is an epiphany for you then let me say it again. <u>The résumé is principally used to eliminate you from consideration!</u> That is its most significant function. You provide the document to someone, they look at it, and drop you from the list. In other words you provide them the bullets to shoot you down.

Nice, huh? But that is what happens hundreds of times before you get a chance at an interview. Remember, hiring is a "last man standing" process, not a "most qualified" process. The reader of that document is looking for a reason to dump you so their job will be easier. So if they are looking for a reason to exile you to oblivion, why would you want to make their job easier? If this screener or reviewer is trying to shoot you down, why would you give him or her the bullets to do so?

So don't fill your résumé with irrelevant garbage! As Joe Friday used to say, "Just the facts, Ma'am." You should present in this document only those things the reader needs to know, and in a format that makes it easier for them to see your credentials.

Sell yourself! Provide a little hype, and good documentation of what you can do for them. Keep it straightforward and simple. Put the most important thing first. Highlight the key skills and strengths the person is looking for. Don't worry about leaving something out. Unless it is relevant, that extra tidbit of too much background might be enough to sink you. Focus on what the reader is looking for, nothing else.

And give them numbers. Cite performance factors with percentages, dollars and volumes. If you do so your document will stand out in the crowd and get a better hearing than other résumés without specific documentation.

Does that help? Is this a revelation for you? Good.

I am not going to address specific formatting for a résumé. I am going to leave that to you. There are hundreds of books out there that show you how to format and write résumés. (I could show you but you would just get bored reading all that stuff.)

Just bear in mind these principles:

1. Focus on the company's requirements, not your background.
2. Run the most important things first.
3. Omit stuff that is not relevant.
4. Sell yourself early on. (this means it needs to sell you before the first fold, in the upper third of the first page.)
5. Don't get buried in the chronology.
6. Cite numbers, dollars, percentages and statistics.

7. Keep the document as crisp as you can, not long winded and tedious.
8. Omit your address. It takes up valuable space at the top of the resume and is not needed.
9. A two-page résumé is usually great. A one-page résumé may be too compact, or too dense, to be easily read, and résumés longer than two pages can be poisonous.
10. Use large print. A document with 10-point type will not be fun to read. Make it 12-point, or even 14.

Generally I would suggest a few specific concepts for composing your resume. Your objective line should be one line no more, and state directly and specifically what you are looking to do. In fact it usually better just to use a targeted job title rather than an objective line. An overview statement of three to six lines should then outline what you are and what you can do. Use bullet statements with key performance factors to reinforce this overview. Your base education or other key credentials should run high in the document without too much detail.

Supplement this with two to three four-line stories indicating your accomplishments, showing the situation you faced, the action you took, and the positive result. The résumé identified should be quantifiable with numbers and percents. It should be easy for the reader to latch on to the performance because you have a specific number in there showing it.

Last, provide a chronology of your last ten to 15 years of work history, with most recent position first. Omit months, show years only. <u>Do not cite "responsibilities", but performance</u>. Wherever possible, hide a break in your employment. Without distorting the truth, try to paint a picture of progression from one position to another.

<u>Leave out things that are not relevant</u>. Remember, a résumé is not an application. As long as it does not mislead the reader, you do not have to include anything you do not want to. Just the facts. Keep it simple.

If you are preparing an initial contact document, just make it readable and ensure it has some eye appeal. For a follow on review document, provide lots of white space and make it pretty. It is usually more traditional to run your education at the end of this document (the follow on résumé) rather than higher up, unless you have virtually no job experience, or the experience you have is not relevant to what you are seeking, but the education is.

Two final points: First, you should make sure the résumé focuses on your objective. If your intent is to be a window washer, the résumé should focus on those aspects of your qualifications that support your washing windows. If your objective is to be the president of a company then your résumé should focus on that objective, demonstrating the talents and skills needed to be an effective company president or senior business leader. If the focus is off, the résumé will fall flat, and will quickly find its way to the circular file.

In this regard, make sure the résumé covers only one or possibly two objectives, not three or four. Don't confuse the reader. Make everything in the résumé point to your key objective.

Second, make sure you include enough empirical supporting information with sufficient data to sell the product (that's you.) Give them performance factors – how well you accomplished something – quantified and supported with specifics and numerical values (percent improvement, money saved, money earned, etc.)

There! Now you know more about résumés than the vast majority of the US population -- including a healthy percentage of recruiters.

One other item that has to be mentioned here. That has to do with the inane tendency among a host of job applicants to want to use "résumé paper" for submitting information to employers or recruiters. You know what stuff I mean. It is the high priced, heavy weight, off color, high grain paper that they sell in office supply or stationery stores. Some people seem convinced this is the stuff an employer wants to see when reviewing your résumé.

Here is why using résumé paper is a stupid practice:

1. It is no longer the standard, so you are wasting your money and energy preparing your presentation materials on expensive paper.
2. Use of résumé paper is passé, no longer in style. If you are using it you are dating yourself, and not delivering the favorable impression you desire by doing so.
3. The classic résumé paper often jams printers, fax machines and even some copiers. Sometimes this stuff will not even absorb your ink, and you will see the ink fleck off the document. Not a very good impression, now is it?
4. The stuff copies poorly. The print does not look as crisp and paper usually does not look as white. It is like smiling with spinach on you teeth.
5. If you send a document on this stuff, especially if you enclose your documents in a "résumé" envelope, it flags to your targeted company that you are sending a résumé. You are inviting them to send the envelope to Human Resources (the bone yard for résumés) without even opening the envelope!

Instead of wasting energy (and money) dealing with the antiquated concept of using résumé paper, just use bright white bond. That is the business standard, and that should be your résumé standard as well.

Now your correspondence arrives at a company looking like regular business correspondence and will be treated as such. This greatly enhances the chances of your documents being reviewed by someone in the company. The paper copies easier and is easier to handle. Plus it will not jam your printer when you are trying to prepare your materials.

Your résumé paper is like your teeth. They look better if they are white and smooth.

Chapter Six

The value of a great letter

A lot of people place too much emphasis on résumés to get them the job. They will spend days fine-tuning the perfect résumé when the résumé itself is often only a secondary tool to marketing yourself for a good position. They agonize over minor points. In some cases they refocus the résumé for submission to each potential position they are going for, expending an exorbitant amount of valuable time with only marginal returns.

Is this the most productive use of your time? Well, as we pointed out before, a résumé is used to eliminate you from consideration more often than not. And although you are expected to have a résumé when presenting your credentials, and having a good résumé can be quite valuable to you, insofar as getting in to see the right person, résumés alone seldom do it for you.

In most businesses inbound résumés are considered the province of Human Resources. All arriving résumés are quickly diverted to HR where they are promptly dispensed with, usually to the shredder. So much for the résumé you spent weeks putting together!

The problem is the résumé just does not penetrate into an organization. Granted, if applying to HR for a position, a résumé is the only thing they want to see. But as we have also learned, applying for "openings" is a minefield fraught with failure.

Instead, every applicant needs to learn the value of a well-written, stand alone business letter. A letter penetrates into an organization better than a résumé. Someone has to open it, digest it, and then route it. This gives you a chance. A good percent of those letters actually end up in the hands of the person they were addressed to. Others end up in the hands of other people in an organization and even if they do not arrive at their intended destination, they can form a basis for a follow up on your part.

A letter can be best used to initiate an informational meeting between you and a person within the company, and as such can get you inside. If you are being referred to this company by someone already inside the company, the letter gives you the opportunity to drop a name (this should be done on the first line.) Then you can move forward in making contact with the people you want to meet.

Usually you begin by asking for a meeting with someone inside the company who is in the know or connected to the decision maker. Or it can go to the decision maker himself, as long as you understand you run the risk here of being excluded from the presence of The Great Oz.

The letter can also address recent goings on within the company, changes, and so forth. When oriented this way it is sometimes called a "situation /opportunity" letter.

If you are pretty sure there is or will be an appropriate opening with this company, you may provide them with a letter-résumé, a document that outlines your credentials in a few paragraphs rather than providing a more tedious résumé. This gives you the chance to put your credentials in the hands of the person making the call instead of counting on HR to get you in to see him or her.

In summary, here are some letter types for you:

1. Informational meeting request. This is sent without a résumé requesting a business meeting. You

are asking for information here. This can be very productive source of leads. (The resultant "business meeting" you have with the person you have addressed is sometimes referred to as an "informational interview".)

2. Direct marketing (to a decision maker.) No résumé is included here either. This letter is sent en lieu of a résumé. It is sometimes called a broadcast letter or letter-résumé. It is very similar to letter requesting an informational meeting, except it contains more stories and a hard citation of your credentials. This is normally sent to targeted employers where it appears there will soon be hiring going on, or where a hiring situation is likely.

With this type of letter it is useful to begin it by discussing a given situation about the company or the industry they are in. You can offer to solve problems arising within the company or address their problems. You can consider whether to use bulleted versus a non-bulleted format. It is critical that you follow up each letter within seven to ten days by phone.

3. Situation or Opportunity Letter. This letter is addressed to the person of interest. Once again this is a stand alone letter sent without résumé. You can use it in conjunction with articles or news items you find about the company, or about individuals you wish to target. This letter cites the news item, then moves or segways into a discussion of the company requirements. Developing such a letter can be both fun and productive.

To decide what to highlight in a situation / opportunity letter, look for changes ongoing or shortly contemplated for the company. These could include:

1. General changes: reorganizations, mergers, changes in senior staff (someone got fired,) layoffs, downsizes, acquisitions, changes in organization, changes in business climate, new contracts, etc.
2. New face: new business, new products, new locations, new branch offices, new competition, new architecture, new technology, new Internet sites;
3. New faces: hiring of a new boss (people on the move,) hiring of office staff, hiring of sales staff, multiple openings, hiring of consultants;
4. Legal activity: bankruptcies, changes in industry standards, new legislation affecting the industry;
5. Finances: acquisition of grants, economic forecasts, company reports, industry reports, etc.

Do you understand how this works now?. The situation / opportunity letter can be used to request an informational interview, or a job interview, depending upon the nature of the intelligence you have access to.

To identify these special opportunities and the basis for much of your writing you will want to watch the business section of the paper, business journals, trades, and other publications to identify what the trends are.

Company websites will sometimes have good information on what is going on as will other web sources.

There are many other types of letters you can use. You should be using thank you letters every time you meet with someone, follow up letters, close follow up letters, third party endorsement letters, and all types of business letters addressed to the people you are trying to see. You will want to have a letter to address to your friends and acquaintances, letters to associations, chambers of commerce, alumni, religious and political leaders, and a plethora of other applications. But most of these can be developed without too much fanfare. There are published sources that can show you how to draft them effectively.

The follow up to an interview letter (best sent via email) is an extremely important document that you must employ. I will discuss this more in the next chapter when we discuss interviewing.

You will notice there is one type of letter that I have not discussed. That is the ubiquitous cover letter. Here is what you need to know:

The principal application of a cover letter for the job seeker is to waste time. That's right. Cover letters are developed for the sole purpose of wasting a lot of time. They waste time for you the job seeker, as well for the person having to read them.

Cover letters are seldom read, although often glanced at. Their only useful function is identifying what position you are interested in, or transmitting your résumé to someone who has requested it already. For these purposes it is all right to use one, but for other purposes, if your résumé is clear enough, the cover letter is mostly redundant and a big drain on your precious time.

If you are using a cover letter as an initial contact document, be prepared for frustration. Using them doesn't help much and is actually counterproductive in most cases because they get between the reader and the thing you want him or her to see, namely the résumé. And, as mentioned, preparing them will bleed away a lot of your time and reduce the effectiveness of your search. You know where that leads don't you? I shudder to think about it.

Granted, a cover letter is nice if you know what job you are going for. A lot of HR departments like to see them. So they could be valuable in some situations. But don't expect the cover letter to be read very often. That being the case, what is it good for? Not much.

When I receive cover letters I throw them in the trash. If I receive them in an email I delete them. Why would a cover letter be needed in conjunction with an email anyway? Isn't that why you type a note into your email itself? Let that be your cover letter! Never attach a cover letter to an email. It just garbages up the process, and in job seeking you need to be crisp, not wordy or overstated. You may think it would be nice if the decision maker had a nice cover letter to look at. But bear in mind, if you attach a résumé to a letter, or attach a letter to a résumé, neither is likely to see the light of day anyway. They all disappear into HR, never to return.

If you intend to use one, I recommend you work at developing a canned cover letter that can be quickly adapted for a variety of situations. You should make sure the letter has no flaws in it. For that reason it should be short and to the point. (If a letter has a mistake in it, it will only make the screener's job easier. He was looking for a reason to drop you out, now he has one.)

In cases where you feel obliged to use one, keep the cover letter short and telegraphic. Don't spend a lot of time on it. Don't put critical information in it. If information about you is important to present, include it in the résumé. But as I implied above, don't depend on the cover letter to help you much! It is usually a throw away document.

Instead, use stand alone letters to make initial contact, not cover letters with résumés. With the stand alone letter you will get shot down with less frequency. The stand alone letter penetrates into the organization better than a résumé and that gives you a chance, which is something you will not have if you are depending on that easily-screened-out résumé to get you in the door.

By the way, if you decide to enclose a cover letter be sure to staple it to the résumé so the two documents do not get separated. The same goes with a letter that extends to a second page. Use a staple and nothing else. Paper clips cause problems when your documents are placed in a stack of other papers.

Chapter Seven

Playing the interview game to win

A lot of people do not know the score with interviewing. I have heard many people say if they can get an interview they can get a job. Sometimes this actually happens. But too much of the time the skilled and practiced interviewee is screened out for one of various oversights.

How long did it take you to get that interview? How many hours, days and weeks did you spend to get in front of the right person? How much money does that represent to you in regard to your time spent and wages not earned? Lots!

Some people feel that since they have a good gift of gab they will naturally do well on an interview.

Sometimes this is far from the truth. In fact the "gift" of gab can be a trap into which many smart but naïve people fall precipitously.

I've heard it said that ancient Sampson was famous for slaying his enemies with the jawbone of an ass. Unfortunately many potential job offers are slain with the same weapon. This is characteristically true of interviewing. The fellow who jaws too much during an interview often opens himself to rejection by the interviewer. He does not understand the rules of the game, does not know the score, and the opposing team wins. Too bad!

Going into an interview with too much confidence or not enough preparation is foolhardy. You must be prepared, you must say the right thing, you must not say the wrong thing, and you must address the needs of the interviewer. You must forget about yourself and think in terms of what is important to the one across the table from you.

Some people feel that if they do well in representing their skills they will secure the job offer. But the process of interviewing people, at least for the initial stage of interviewing, is just like résumé screening. It is a process of elimination. That is, the interviewer is looking for a reason to eliminate the applicant. If the interviewer perceives a weakness in qualification, and can find a good reason to not hire this person, the applicant is flushed into Never Land.

And the best or strongest applicant? Sometimes a truly well qualified person, who can present his or her skills effectively, will survive this initial interview process. But all too frequently the person being interviewed divulges something that could be perceived as a weakness. Or the interviewer identifies something that is a concern. So long! You are gone.

This very qualified candidate, who is sometimes someone who could make a big difference in the company that is hosting the interviews, is promptly eliminated like everyone who went before. Why? Simple. A liability (or perceived liability) was surfaced, and that makes it easy for the interviewer to eliminate another victim.

Lets dissect the interview process to better understand what is going on here. There are three important aspects to a successful interview. First, selling your credentials in such a way that you impress the interviewer. Second, addressing liabilities, whether perceived or real, successfully. Third, building rapport. In each of these aspects one has to address the needs of the interviewer, not the requirements for the position, or one's qualifications.

I will talk about each of these things individually. But first we need to understand about interview stages.

Because knowing what stage you are in will help you understand what the interviewer wants to see, and how to address the needs of the interviewer during the process.

There are usually three stages to the interview process. These are the initial screening stage, the reinforcement stage, and the late stage, or final selection stage. Sometimes each of these stages is represented by one interview. Sometimes one interview can cover all three stages. Less often there can be multiple interviews in each stage.

The screening stage is a continuation of the résumé review process. The assigned interviewer takes the list of perceived qualified candidates and runs through each of them in a qualifying interview with the intent of narrowing the list down. This is done by discussing the résumé in depth with the applicant, or qualifying the résumé, and then recertifying the individual being considered as qualified.

Qualifying the résumé is essentially a review of one's tangible assets and how they gel in regard to the position at hand. To qualify the résumé the interviewer will probe aspects of the résumé to insure the résumé is an accurate representation of the applicant's qualifications, and measuring the depth of those qualifications with leading questions.

The questions could be something like, "How long did you work for McCurdy Engineering?" "Was that before or after you left Jones Architects?" "How many people did you supervise, how big was your budget, and what were your key responsibilities?"

The interviewer is probing to insure you are qualified for the position in question. The basis of this stage of interviews is a review of "tangible assets." These are assets or skills that can be measured. They are generally reflected in the résumé, or else they are implied in the résumé. Your tangible assets might include who the former employer was, what line of business they were in, how much responsibility did you have, and how closely aligned are your outward qualifications to those recited for this position.

In conjunction with qualifying the résumé, the interviewer will also recertify the person. That is, he or she will ascertain whether there are any obvious distortions with the résumé, and whether the applicant has any discernable liabilities or disqualifiers.

Sometimes the certification process can happen very early in the screening interview, and can be over with in a hurry. The interviewer may ask how much you want to make, or how soon you are available to go to work. If either of these answers puts you outside the parameters they are working with, the interview is suddenly over. These may be the first screening questions asked. If you give the wrong answer the conversation is over, and you are yesterday's leftovers. Good bye!

This type of screening will normally be conducted over the phone. This initial phone interview can be over with in a few seconds, or it could extend to 20 or 30 minutes, depending upon what the principal qualifying and certifying criteria for the position are, and how the interviewer wants to proceed.

Phone interviewing can be difficult because one does not have the privilege of looking the other person in the eye. But it can be advantageous to the one being interviewed. For one, you are not being evaluated based upon clothing or appearance. Second you can make ample use of cheat sheets or reference documents, and third you can participate in the interview from the comfortable surroundings of your own home or office.

Early in-person screening interviews are usually tightly scheduled and conducted in the offices of the interviewing company. Usually they last only a few minutes, and first impressions carry the day. Sometimes the applicants are gathered for a group interview. Often each will be asked to complete an application, if one has not already been tendered previously.

These activities are used to eliminate lesser qualified candidates or ones who have issues so the follow-on interviews can be conducted efficiently. Filling out an application is an important task. Usually there are questions on the application designed to make it easier for the screener to cull you out.

Questions such as salary and compensation, who you worked for, and what your duties were, etc., tend to show up, and the screener then can refer to these along with the résumé to see who to drop from the list. Then at the bottom you have to sign that these things are precise and accurate. Any omissions that are discovered later on can be grounds for dismissal.

The survivors of the screening interview are usually passed at this point to a reinforcement type of interview. This is a face to face interview usually taking 20 to 45 minutes. Its purpose is to fine tune the screening process in order to develop a list of finalists to go forward to a decision maker.

Although rapport building is important throughout the interview process, this is probably the first place in the interviewing process where establishing rapport becomes vital. The interviewer is mostly searching for key qualifications, or probing for disqualifiers, but the interviewer can also be influenced by whether he or she likes this person or not. If no serious liabilities have surfaced, and if remaining liabilities are quieted, and if the overt qualifications for the position are being addressed, then the interviewer may simply rate the survivors based upon whether he or she likes them.

The final stage interview is generally conducted by someone higher up in the organization. This is frequently the person who will be the hiree's supervisor, or someone at a higher level. For executive positions this interview will invariably be conducted by a senior executive with the firm.

The agenda for this type of interview is usually based on personal rapport and company culture. The interviewer is trying to determine whether the person being interviewed is a fit for the culture, and whether he or she wants to work with the one being interviewed.

Key factors being evaluated include a person's attitude and his or her personal qualities. Disqualifiers might be a haughty attitude, an overbearing personality, or an inability to express oneself effectively. Another important factor being considered is your level of enthusiasm for the position for which you are being considered.

If you are being taken through the interview process by a recruiter, you will often be subjected to the first stages of the interview by the recruiter himself. When you finally end up speaking to a representative of the company you are usually in a final stage interview.

Selling yourself, addressing liabilities, and building rapport are important at each stage of the interview. Rapport building becomes most critical in a late stage interview. But it can be helpful at any interview stage, and sometimes can help you salvage an interview that you might otherwise have failed. Lack of the ability to build rapport early on can certainly sink you.

Once, when I worked for the Colorado Department of Labor & Employment my team was assigned the responsibility of hiring a colleague. My team assigned me the responsibility of conducting the telephonic screening of applicants, and then we brought all the ones who passed this screening into an interview. We conducted the interview by panel, that is, three of us together interviewed each person at the same time.

The person I felt was best qualified when I had spoken to her by phone arrived on time, but wanted to provide each member of the panel with some supporting information (these were a series of letters of recommendation I believe.) So she asked the person at the reception desk to make copies of this documentation.

The receptionist that day was also a member of our team, and since the three of us were tied up in interviews, she was quite busy. When the applicant asked for her materials to be copied, the team member asked her to wait while she took care of pressing business.

The applicant, instead of waiting patiently, tore into the team member for not helping her out. Ouch! She finally got her copies, then came in for the interview.

The applicant interviewed very well and convinced us she was very well qualified. She also presented herself very well, and we all liked her. All of us, that is, except for the poor overwhelmed member of our team that had been covering the front desk. After the interview she explained to us what type of personality we were dealing with, and we happily chose another applicant for the position.

This type of thing happens all the time. People do not recognize who may have a vote in the interview and quickly get themselves shot down due to a lapse in observance of protocol, or failure to pay attention to rapport building.

I will address the handling of liabilities in a subsequent section. Let's talk for a moment about selling your credentials.

You are now in front of the interviewer who is trying to determine who to send forward to the boss for final interview. What is the purpose of this interview? What is the interviewer trying to achieve?

The purpose is simple. The interviewer is trying to narrow the list, so is looking for reasons to eliminate candidates. That's right. The purpose of most interviews is the same as with the résumé screening process. The last man standing concept is still in force. But also, the interviewer is trying to identify someone with good credentials.

So from your perspective, what should your goal be? First, to not get eliminated. That means showing yourself as a professional, well qualified candidate with no disqualifiers, or serious liabilities.

At this point a disqualifier would be a poor employment record, a serious lack of qualifications for the position, or something glaringly damaging about your background.

I remember interviewing an applicant for a position managing our company's distribution center. One candidate was very well qualified, intelligent and capable. He was also easy to like. But the man weighed over 300 lbs. and looked as old as the Republic of Texas. I was afraid he was going to keel over from a heart attack right in front of me. Despite his generally good qualifications, he had a glaring problem, and that was an apparent lack of good health.

So if you have no disqualifiers at this point, what would be termed a liability? This could be anything that could be discerned as making you less qualified than others being considered. This could include lesser experience, wrong background, limited education, or possibly an issue from a previous employment, such as termination for cause, etc.

But how about selling your credentials? How are you going to convince the interviewer that you have top notch credentials? Very simple. You are going to illustrate them. What does that mean? That means providing a series of illustrative examples of your performance vis-à-vis the requirements needed for the position. You are going to identify the asset the interviewer is looking for, and cite an example of how you have used that asset or qualification to produce a positive result. Here is an example.

Question: "Mr. Smith, it says on your résumé you have cost control experience."

Response query: "That's true I have had a variety of experience in cost control. What aspect of cost control is most important to you?"

Clarification question: "Well, have you ever developed a plan for controlling costs in a manufacturing setting?"

Answer with story: "Yes I have. When I was with ABC company I discovered our production costs were 10 to 20% higher than normal. So I gathered input from the staff as to our costs incurred in raw materials, labor, and distribution. I discovered our floor production efficiency was less than optimal, and many of our raw materials costs were higher than necessary.

"So I developed a plan for acquisition of raw materials that permitted me to identify the lowest cost supplier. I also employed techniques for reducing the number of personnel involved in the production process. I incorporated these corrections into a plan that provided standard guidance on both acquisition and production processes."

"As the company implemented my plan, costs were reduced between 12 and 15% and profit margins went up nearly 5%."

Reconfirmation: "Is that the type of cost control activity you are seeking?"

Interviewer's confirmation: "Yes, Mr. Smith. That is what I was looking for."

Naturally, not every discussion on your qualifications will be quite this straightforward, but the basic idea here is to site specific examples, preferably in story format, that illustrate your assets to the interviewer.

Once you have done that with each asset of interest, you have filled the interviewer's slate with positive check marks, and you have most likely survived the process.

The next thing you need to do is identify any problems or liabilities. You can do this by watching the interviewer's response to your answers, or even better, by asking the interviewer specifically what your limitations are. This could go something like this:

"Ms. Jones, what concerns do you have about my qualifications for this position?"

Or you could say, "What would you consider to be the biggest obstacles to my being able to secure this position? What do you think I lack in order to do the job?"

Once you have identified the interviewer's concern, you should then determine what the basis of this concern is. This might go like this.

Concern: "I am concerned you do not have specific experience in managing a warehouse of this size."

Acknowledgement: "I am glad we have a chance to discuss this."

Basis: "If I understand the basis of your concern, you want to make sure the person hired can handle assets of the magnitude you are dealing with in this facility. Is that correct?"

Confirmation: "Yes, we want to make sure you can deal with the problems associated with this level of position."

Test question: "If I can demonstrate that I have this level of experience, would you be satisfied with my qualifications for this position?"

Confirmation: "Naturally."

Applicable story: "Let me give you an example of my qualification in this regard. When I was with XYZ I was the Assistant Manager of a warehouse with over 200,000 square feet, that involved the loading and dispatch of as many as 12 trucks per day, and the processing of four railcar loads of raw materials each evening. In this capacity I built processes and programs that increased efficiency 10 to 20%, permitting us to conduct operations with 10 fewer people per shift."

Qualification: "Does this help you see how I can function well in an environment with large capacity warehouse operations?"

Resolution: "Yes, I am now satisfied with your credentials in this area."

At this point in the conversation you can inquire about other concerns the interviewer may have, and then move on to discuss other aspects of the job that dictate the type of experience or qualifications you possess.

If at any point in the above process you determine the interviewer is not convinced, then you should return to the basis of the concern and rephrase it.

Restate: "I may have misunderstood. Does the actual basis of your concern have more to do with the type of warehouse operation I worked in, or the size of the operation?"

Clarification: "No, I am only concerned about your experience in preparing freight for air shipment."

Redirect: "Very well, may I address this? When I was with QWT freight I was supervisor of air freight operations, and grew operations from one truck load to three truckloads a day without a loss of efficiency or raising costs. Does this ease your concern?"

Confirmation. "Yes, I see that you are qualified in this area."

Naturally you will want to develop a number of adaptations to this question and answer process. But once you have the concept, you should be able to address almost all liabilities, assuming you can recite enough of the right type of specific examples and the stories they apply to.

By now you should have been able to address the company requirements, quieted perceived liabilities, and built rapport with the interviewer and anyone else you have been in contact with.

After the interview you must send a follow up letter, preferably by email. In this letter you should thank the interviewer for the opportunity to meet with them (if more than one interviewer, then send a separate email to each one.) You should then reemphasize the aspects of the interview you want to make sure are pointed out. You should definitely express enthusiasm for the company and for the position you were being considered for.

This letter is also an opportunity to address anything discussed in the interview that may not have gone as well as hoped, perhaps by answering a certain question more fully, or adding something you forgot to include in the conversation. The tone of the letter should be upbeat, positive and to the point.

Chapter Eight

Negotiating for advantage

Something we have not yet addressed in our allegory is the need to negotiate a prenuptial contract with the princess before you marry her. After all, there are lands properties, possessions and royalties on the table that need to be carefully ascribed to the appropriate heirs.

Metaphorically the "pre-nup" represents the job offer. Once you have an offer, there is a definite need to negotiate the conditions of your employment instead of letting the employer dictate all the terms.

Some people never think about negotiating a job offer. They take the offer on face value, start work and are content. That is unless they discover one of their peers has a sweeter deal than they do.

The point of all this is that you get the best situation from a given position by successfully negotiating the terms of your employment before you ever start the job. Once again, the best job does not necessarily go to the best qualified. Nor is the best qualified the one that gets the best deal. Although qualifications can certainly help, when it comes to positioning yourself for the best advantage in a given employment situation, the laurels often go to the one who knows how to negotiate successfully.

The first thing to ask yourself as you ponder the receipt of an offer is what you are worth. You need to understand that your real value to a company can vary dramatically from company to company, depending on what their requirements are and what you can bring to the table.

Another aspect of your value has to do with what you will accept. You may think that what you are worth is defined as what you can get as an offer. From the employer's perspective, however, even if you are worth a great deal, if they feel you will accept a certain amount, then that is all you will probably see in the offer.

What it really comes down to is you do not necessarily get what you are worth, but in the final outcome you get what you can negotiate.

A lot of people do not understand the value of negotiating an offer. And for lesser paying positions typically there is not a lot to negotiate. But even with a lesser position, often times you can at least improve your working conditions if you ask before accepting the position.

You may be able to cite examples, however, of people who have tried to negotiate an offer and failed. The tendency is to think there is no possibility of negotiating. In most cases it merely means that the other party (the employer) was a better negotiator.

Let's look at it this way, if a company wants to hire you, don't you think they have a vested interest in having a happy employee? Of course they do! And if they bring you on board in a way that insures you are happy working there it is only in their best interest.

The key to the whole process is how you negotiate. Many people when negotiating make mistakes that destroy their negotiating position, or end the negotiations altogether.

There are three common mistakes that job seekers typically make in a negotiation. If you can avoid these mistakes, chances are you will have a successful negotiation.

These are:

1. Wrong tone: the negotiation gets off to a bad footing or a good tone is not maintained, and the process comes unraveled.

2. Cart before the horse: this means items to negotiate are presented in the wrong sequence, and this causes misunderstandings, and the process becomes stymied.

3. Failure to get something in writing. This means not starting out with a written document, and then failing to get something you have negotiated properly documented for future reference.

Let's talk about these for a moment.

Wrong tone: The nature and tone of the compensation negotiation must always be soft. The tone should be conciliatory and congenial. There should be no hard language.

You should regard a negotiation as similar to a prenuptial agreement. (Remember the Sleeping Beauty example -- for a royal wedding a "pre-nup" is often necessary.) With this type of agreement, you do not want to tick off the other party because you have to live with them later. So you approach the negotiation very softly, and in a professional manner.

In this vein you can technically ask for almost anything, as long as you demand nothing. Let me say that again: Ask for anything, but demand nothing. Do you catch the concept? You can ask for any number of things as long as your tone is sweet and congenial, and you do not come across as demanding.

Once you start demanding certain things, you can kill the deal. You could be perceived as mercenary and not a team player. Or they can feel that you do not want the job that badly. This often results in the offer being withdrawn. At a minimum they will simply tell you no, and the negotiation is pretty much over.

Another aspect of the tone is the value of vulnerability. Some people think if they are negotiating they need to stand tough. This is not so when it comes to compensation negotiations. You are being offered a job. They are the ones picking up the tab. They have all the marbles. So you must be able to negotiate from a position of weakness and must be willing to demonstrate your vulnerability. Showing vulnerability is advantageous because you are able to get more that way than you would be able to otherwise.

There is a story from ancient times in which a Roman cohort arrives at a village in Gaul. The Romans are on a war footing, and upon arrival immediately demand to see the village elders. The Roman leader establishes his position by pointing out to the village elders that they are on a pillaging mission and that the Gauls are their enemies.

The Romans state their conditions: the Gauls must become their slaves and all their property is to be confiscated. Those who are too old to serve in slavery (like the village elders) will simply be put on a pike and that will be the end of it.

The elders hold a rapid crisis meeting. Their options are not good. But they figure they would be better off opposing the Romans than submitting to them outright. So they get their swords, their pitchforks and their slings, call their young men out of the fields, and go after the Romans.

The Roman soldiers are professionals however. They know their business, and after a short battle, the village elders are all rounded up and placed on pikes, the young men who survive the battle become Roman slaves and the women ... oh, well. The village property is confiscated and what is remaining of the village is burned.

A few days later the Roman cohort comes to another village of Gauls, and delivers the same ultimatum. Do as we demand or else! The village elders get together in a hurried meeting and try to determine what to do. They have heard about what has happened to the previous village and realize that "resistance is futile."

Then one of them comes up with a new approach. How about if we simply beg for mercy?

So they send for their fair daughters and the young wives of the village, have them clean up a bit and send them out to meet with the Romans. The women throw themselves on the mercy of the Romans and beg them to spare their village. "Please do not slay our brothers, our husbands and fathers!" they cry.

The Romans are a bit smitten by the women and consider the petition. The pitiful pleas of the defenseless women have an impact on them. Since they are tired and weary of so much pillaging anyway, they decide to acquiesce.

Meanwhile the village elders have prepared a feast for their Roman visitors, and now invite them into the main plaza. There the Romans eat the fatted calf and get drunk on French wine. While they are still in a good mood the whole village escorts the visitors out of town.

The moral? When you are in a vulnerable position you do better by showing vulnerability than trying to be tough. This is especially true of compensation negotiations. In compensation negotiations you should always negotiate from a position of weakness, not strength.

Here is a way you could express it to the person making the offer: "You know, Tony, I have never negotiated an offer quite like this one and I am really at a loss as to what to do."

Tony then sees you as someone who is reasonable and cooperative, and he lowers his guard. He no longer is protecting his company from a materialistic predator, but he is seeing you now as someone who merely wants a fair shake. So he is willing to listen to your request. If he feels your request is reasonable, he will likely grant it in the interest of establishing a good working relationship with you.

Let's talk about the cart before the horse. In compensation negotiations it is vital for you to deal with things in proper sequence. If you go into an interview with a list of wants, or end up discussing compensation before an offer is tendered, you will be regarded as unprofessional, mercenary or a little naïve. None of these places you in a good position to negotiate anything. If you do this, chances are you will never survive the interview process, and not receive the offer anyway.

You should never discuss money, terms or conditions before you have an offer in hand. To do otherwise is suicide.

In negotiating an offer you need to wait to discuss matters until after they are prepared to extend an offer, and before you get into a discussion about it. Otherwise you could lose out entirely.

If they ask you how much money you have been making, it will be hard to avoid telling them. But just don't get into a discussion of what you are worth until after you see something from them in writing.

Once you get into the negotiation you should observe the four stages. These are, the preliminary stage, the query, the response and the meeting.

The <u>preliminary stage</u> is when you first receive the offer from them. At this point there is only one thing you do and that is tell them how excited you are to receive the offer. Now practice this out loud, "I'm soooo excited!" No, with more gusto. Try it again, only this time say it like you mean it. "I'm extremely excited about this offer !!!!" That's better.

Once you have put them at ease regarding your willingness to work for hem, you are in business. Anything less and they could come away from the process a bit offended that you did not regard the offer as all that desirable. Please bear in mind that they may have spent quite a bit of time putting a nice offer together for you. Don't offend them by not showing how excited you are about it!

The <u>query stage</u> is where you find out what the offer consists of. You are not negotiating anything here, just asking questions. This is where you find out about the company benefits package, whether there is a company bonus plan, etc. If you need to you may need to get an appointment with Human Resources to gather up all the details. You should normally ask these questions in a professional, deferential email

The <u>response stage</u> is when you respond to the offer. If you are being offered a standard package for a lower management or non-management position, you will probably not need to provide them a written response. However if you are a mid-level manager, an executive or professional you will want to respond to their offer in writing to avoid miscues.

In this response you are identifying what things you wish to negotiate. You are setting an agenda for what you would like to speak with them about regarding the offer. If you are going for a junior position there may not be much to negotiate here. But for a more senior position, your wish list may include four to five items you want to speak about. (If you can limit your list to three that is better.)

You are basically saying here, "These are the things I would like to discuss." But you will use a softer tone. You might say it like this, "Do you think we could discuss these items further? They are very important to me, and I am confident we can come to an agreement on them."

Your response, once again, should be presented in a professional, deferential email. You must ask, not demand, and be sure to ask nicely!

The meeting is when you discuss the particulars with whoever is handling the negotiation with you, either in person or by phone. This is where the "agenda" you provided them can be very helpful. Naturally you very rarely get everything you want, but if you negotiate smartly with the right attitude you will get a lot more than you would have had you not negotiated with them.

Remember to keep the tone soft, ask nicely, show vulnerability, be agreeable, and cite good realistic reasons for your position on a given item. If you are reasonable about something you are more likely to get what you requested.

Getting everything in writing is important. It will come back to haunt you later if you do not have everything put to print. You need to begin the negotiation process with a written document. An email is sufficient here. But you want to be able to start the process with an offer document that can be read. This keeps things from moving around during the process, and also gives you a point of reference to begin discussion.

After you have negotiated the offer successfully, you will want the terms and conditions ironed out and put to writing. You should not accept a verbal agreement for anything that is of importance. Most of us do not live in West Texas, so a handshake just isn't good enough!

Why? Think about it. Is the person who is extending you promises or assurances going to remember them the way you will a couple of years from now. Won't this person be more apt to side with the company on an issue regarding what you were offered?

Is this person always going to be with the company, and will they stick up for you if you need to work something out later? If you cannot answer with an absolute yes, make sure you get everything <u>of any importance whatever</u> put down in hard copy and keep it where you can find it when you need it. If you don't you could end up being real sorry later on!

If they do not provide this, then you should send them a polite message with what you understand they have agreed to. Save the email. Then you will have a record to go back to later on if needed.

Here are some of the items that could go into your compensation package:

Base salary: This is what a lot of people think of as what they are actually making. But for executives and professionals, one should also expect to see bonuses, severance agreements and possibly equities in the mix.

Bonuses: A bonus could include a sign on bonus, or an incentive payment to get you to accept the offer. It would likely include an annual bonus (sometimes paid quarterly) that is usually based on a combination of individual performance as well as company performance. (You normally see a bonus arrangement for mid-level managers on up.) In some cases a signing bonus may be in order as well.

You will want to find out when you are querying the offer what the chances are of you receiving any bonus, and what it would take for you to get it. You also want to ask what percent of people working at your level received a bonus last year. (If no one is actually receiving a bonus, even though they say they have a bonus program, there isn't really a bonus included, now is there?)

Position Description: When receiving an offer you will definitely want to request a position description for the job you are going to do, as well as a reporting structure outlining who reports to whom. This is crucial!

Why do you need this? Because your compensation package is directly related to the job you are doing. If you do not have documentation as to the job you are going to be doing, what the responsibilities are and who you are reporting to, etc., the position could change once you start working. Once the position changes, so does your compensation, and all the things you just negotiated are out the window.

You may think this strange, but I have seen this happen before. A person thinks he is being hired for position X but when he shows up for his first day of work he finds out they have changed everything and he now has position Y. In some cases the last minute changes are innocuous or sometimes good, but often times they can be devastating to you and your career. Make sure you get ALL of it in writing before you sign an acceptance, and this includes a complete description of the position you are being offered.

Terms, conditions and expectations of employment: It is important to understand what will be expected of you, especially if this is not clarified in the job description. How much travel will be required if you accept the job? What hours will you be working, and on what schedule, etc.?

Vacation: How much vacation will you be able to expect the first year, and when will you be able to take it? How many sick days or personal days are generally allowed? Which holidays will the company observe?

Relocation: What is included and not included in the relocation package? What will they pay for and how will payment be addressed? Will they be paying mileage reimbursement? If so, at what rate? Will you be allowed to direct bill the company for your moving costs, will they pay it directly, or will you have to pay for this and request reimbursement later? How about temporary storage of household goods or temporary lodging while you find a place to live?

Salary review: How often will you be receiving a salary and performance review, and what are the criteria your performance will be judged on? What will any increases be based on? How soon can you expect to receive your first review?

Start date: This is a negotiable item. You may need to request a start date that is amenable to your personal situation.

On another subject, I sometimes get queries from people who have competing offers. In other words, what if more than one company has tendered you an offer? Although it is rare that this occurs, this can be a very desirable condition to be in. But please bear in mind that many companies do not like to compete so be very judicious in how you handle this. If you tell one company you have a competing offer they will sometimes simply withdraw their offer and move on to another candidate on their list.

Having a second offer come in at the same time you are working the first is great. Just tread lightly, and negotiate the best delay you can. If possible try to stall on the offer that seems less desirable, then negotiate the preferred offer successfully.

Avoid letting too much time pass. If you have a legitimate offer, you need to move forward with it as quickly as possible, otherwise the offer could be withdrawn, or if there is a second one pending, the first one could disappear.

One other matter of vital importance here is being able to distinguish between an offer and an expression of interest. I know of people who turned off a real offer that was brewing because they thought they were getting an offer from another company, only to discover the second offer never materialized. In the meantime the offer they actually had vanished. Ouch!

Now, having gained an understanding of some basic principles of negotiating you are much better prepared to negotiate for advantage. You will never know everything there is to know about negotiating, and there is a lot more that could be said on the subject, but if you keep these principles in mind as you approach an offer, you will be in a much better position to improve your compensation or working conditions.

Remember, if you do not ask, you do not get. Second, you can ask for anything, but demand nothing. Lastly, be sure to get it all down on paper!

Chapter Nine

Recruiters: The good, the bad, the indifferent

One day a few years ago someone came into my office confident he would get a job. He wanted some new leads just in case, but he was not worried he would land something soon. I asked him why he felt things were going well for him. "I have three recruiters working for me," he naively declared.

I just shook my head. I don't remember if this fellow ever got a job. He probably did eventually. But I can assure you he did not get one through a recruiter.

If you have a recruiter working for you, you are an employer, not a job seeker. Employers are the ones who pay recruiters. So that's who the recruiters work for. If you have spoken to a recruiter who has assured you he or she would help you get a job, you have just been hoodwinked by a used car salesman. Recruiters may be courteous and professional. (Some are, some are not.) But they are never working for you unless you are paying them something. (And heaven forbid that you should!) Any information to the contrary is a deception.

There are generally four types of recruiters. All of them work for the employer, or the person within a given company looking for talent.

The first type of recruiter (sometimes called a staffing manager) is an employee on salary with the company doing the hiring. This person may be part of the Human Resources department, or, if with a larger company, may belong to a recruiting department all on its own. Though this individual may earn bonuses if achieving certain recruiting goals, he or she generally receives the same base salary whether or not a given position is filled. Typically this type of recruiter is methodical and task oriented, because that is the typical profile of an HR technician.

Though they must be able to perform their job, staffing managers are typically not people who are taught to think outside the box, nor would they normally be permitted to do so. They respond to the tasking given to them in a given week, and perform systematically the duties associated with their job description.

The second type of recruiter works with some type of employment agency. They typically specialize in administrative, technical or low level management positions. Many of which are in the temporary hire business. Most of them can't help you, unless you are in a specific occupation or industry segment this agency specializes in, are interested in a temporary or entry-level position, or are interested in one of those jobs no one else wants.

The third type of recruiter is retained. That is, they serve under a retainer to one or several companies. Their focus is to recruit high paid executives or difficult to fill, well paid professional positions. They are usually paid the same amount whether they place someone in a position or not. They merely respond to the tasking of the person who has retained them, presenting the best candidates they can muster for a given opening to the representative of the company retaining them.

Most retained recruiters are experts in their field or industry. Many of them are executives or professionals who have served in the field or industry they are recruiting in. They tend to be intimate with the characteristics of the industries they work with and the companies represented in that industry. They not only know the companies retaining them, but also the chief competitors within the industry, and many of the leaders making a mark in the industry.

Retained recruiters are, for the most part, motivated to represent their company well and the client companies who have retained them. Because of that, they will often conduct public relations while they recruit. They tend to say positive things about their clients and will rarely say anything negative to an applicant. They want to maintain a strong reputation in their field and do not want people to think ill of them or the people they represent.

The word of caution here is that they will tend to put a positive spin on things, and thus sometimes unintentionally mislead the candidates they are working with. But rarely will a retained recruiter intentionally mislead people. Unless, of course, he is misrepresenting the value of his services to an employer.

The fourth type of recruiter is the contingency recruiter. A contingency recruiter often focuses on mid-level managers, specialized professionals, engineers, and sometimes higher paid executives. To comprehend what the agenda is here it is important to understand how a contingency recruiter makes money.

A contingency recruiter is normally working for commission. He or she works to secure a contract with a company in their area of focus, then address the company requirements. He or she will work with a variety of client companies to convince them to list an opening with him, or in some cases merely to identify the type of people a given company tends to be looking for. Once he succeeds, he will employ various methods to identify candidates. Many times he is working with candidates he has already worked with in the past. He will screen the ones identified and select the ones he feels will most likely be received favorably by his client.

At that point he will conduct a screening interview with a prospective candidate, satisfy himself as to their potential, and present the best he has to his client for consideration. The person with the opening at the client company will then usually interview at least some of the candidates presented and decide whether to hire one of them or not.

If one of the recruiter's candidates is hired, the recruiter will collect a commission, usually equal to between 20% and 30% of the salary of the person hired.

As you can see, an effective contingency recruiter who is diligent and focused can usually make a decent income. But as you can also see, the contingency recruiter sometimes has no incentive to remain above board in his relationship with job candidates. His motivation is to secure a paid for placement, and that is sometimes his only motivation.

The reason I can say this is that I myself have worked as a contingency recruiter. Now many contingency recruiters are extremely professional, including me. They deal in repeat business with a number of client companies and are extremely conscientious in the way they handle assignments. They also work hard to maintain a positive image in the eyes of the candidates they work with. In fact many recruiters who serve on contingency will also have retainers with certain companies, and thus work both types of searches, retained and contingency.

Then there are the other guys. Some contingency recruiters are simply not very honest. They are the snake oil salesmen of the business. (I know that because I compete against some of these types regularly.) They will sometimes readily allow a candidate to believe things that are not true about the potential employer, and will sometimes outright deceive people about the nature of opportunities available. Since they are only interested in seeing a match occur they will sometimes force a match. That is, arrange for an applicant to be placed in a position that is either not right for the company or not right for the candidate.

As a candidate you should be aware of what you are up against when dealing with these guys. Just because a recruiter says it doesn't mean it is so. The position he is pitching may not be right for you, even though it may sound good at first. The recruiter may have you over a barrel if he can get you to believe his story about the virtues of a given position.

Once you have accepted it you are rarely in a position to make a break from the job until after several months have passed, and you could then be stuck in a disappointing situation with accompanying unpleasant long term consequences. In the meantime your contingency recruiter has collected his commission.

So how do you tell the difference between a retained (usually professional) and a contingency recruiter? And how can you distinguish between a good, professional contingency recruiter and a not so good, unprofessional one?

Sometimes it is not easy to tell. Because a contingency recruiter may tell you he is on retainer when he is not. But go ahead and ask him. "Is this a retained search, or a contingency assignment?" If he refuses to answer, then he is a contingency recruiter. If he admits he is a contingency recruiter he may be honest about other things and you will probably be all right.

Another way to tell what type of recruiter you are working with is his pace of operation. The classic contingency recruiter will be talking fast, and will have something to sell. Most people can tell if they are being sold something, and you will be able to pick up on the tone of the conversation. The retained recruiter on the other hand is not in a big hurry because he is most interested in creating a good match, and because he wants his client to be happy.

A contingency recruiter will often conduct initial phone screenings with two to three questions, then press on to the next candidate. If you are the person getting screened you could experience an interview that can last less than 30 seconds. Wow!

The reason the contingency recruiter is in a hurry is because he is in competition with other recruiters. Companies who contract with contingency recruiters will often give their listing to more than one agency. This means the recruiter that calls you is sometimes competing with one or more other recruiters for the same business, hence the hurry. Once he has a screened list to work with, he presents the list to his client. If one of those people is hired he can claim the commission.

The retained folks are not competing with anyone. They are already receiving a retainer, and will take their time when they contact you. They already have a contract with their client, and are charging the client an enormous sum for their activity.

So, if you can get your credentials in front of the right recruiter you have a chance at a good job, right? Wrong!

Most recruiters do not want to talk with you because in most cases you do not have what they want. That's right. You are not what they are looking for. What do I mean by that?

Why do you think a recruiter is hired, anyway? He is given the assignment because he can identify people who have "sought after" credentials. If you do not have the credentials that people are looking for you will not be speaking with a recruiter for very long. They will be focused on talking with other folks, the people with hot credentials. A recruiter does not have a basket of jobs he or she is handing out! He is out rounding up special types of people who are marketable to his clients. Everyone else needs to look elsewhere.

So what is it that recruiters want? A few main qualifications, or some specialized qualifications. That's all. To candidates not in possession of these special qualifications he or she will be mostly indifferent.

One thing a recruiter may be looking for is fast track youth. This is the young fast-moving hot shot that went to one of those name brand colleges, and now has five to ten years of business experience under his belt. This person is marketable because a lot of companies want to create a brain trust of capable and productive young executives.

The second thing they may be after is turnaround experts. A turnaround expert is someone who has the ability to take a poorly performing company and make it productive. Usually this person has "C"-level experience. This means someone who has been a CEO, CFO, COO or CMO (or possibly a Senior VP for Sales) before, and has a track record of turning around company performance. (If you don't know what the acronyms stand for, don't worry about it. You aren't one of these people, so relax.)

Third, a recruiter most often wants a person with very specialized experience. This is probably the most common situation. Maybe it's someone who has unique business talent, one who speaks a foreign language, has specialized certifications or has worked in a unique industry situation. Many types of engineers are in demand these days. Highly technical petroleum or mining engineers are always in demand, as are people with technological backgrounds. The target is normally someone that may be hard to find, and so a recruiter is put on the task to find this person with the unique skills or qualifications.

This means if you are not one of the types of people the recruiter normally looks for, oh well! They want those people with unique, in-demand skills. The recruiter is rarely looking for someone like you, and can therefore do nothing for you. Hence, his attitude of apparent indifference toward you.

And where do recruiters go to find qualified people for the positions he is filling? Frequently they will pull résumés from a job board. But the primary source is very simple. They will often source (as in "steal") them from a competing company. That's right, they call a company, and talk to someone in a position at the same level as the position they are trying to fill. Then they convince them to cough up a résumé, and the game is on. They can do something similar with people they find on LinkedIn, or on other professional networks

This means recruiters are less likely to be dealing with a stack of résumés of people who are out of work. They are instead involved in a walnut shell game of moving employed people back and forth between positions in different companies. Some people go their entire careers without ever having to look for a job because the job comes to them. And the delivery man is a recruiter.

Despite what people may think a recruiter is up to, as I mentioned above, recruiters do not work for applicants or job candidates. They are invariably paid by the employer, and are responsive to their clients, the people who are paying them, and no one else. If you are not what they are looking for, they will be able to do nothing for you, and your expectation of getting a job through one of them is a vain hope.

Nevertheless recruiters often provide job seeking information. They will sometimes offer suggestions to people who are in the market for employment and are sometimes held up as gurus in the business. I have been astounded at the number of people who fall down at the feet of recruiters because they feel they know everything there is to know about the job market. This is foolhardy.

Recruiters in many cases know no more than you do about the job market. They have a limited amount of information on the market in general and are often only experts in the field or industry in which they recruit. They can tell you what they like to see in a résumé but can't tell you with any real precision what you need to have in the résumé to get a job.

I have had recruiters working for me that were totally incompetent, and I unfortunately had to dismiss them. Hopefully people they spoke to were not relying on them for career advice!

Additionally, since recruiters are generally looking for special kinds of people, they have a limited understanding of the overall job market. They are only seeing a portion of the market, so are seeing things from a limited perspective. In addition, much of their activity involves talking with people who are working, and not with those who are out looking for a job.

Sometimes recruiters can be a good source of information on their principal market, and you should not hesitate to speak with one about what they know the most. Bear in mind they are seeing things at the tail end of the market trend, after a job has already been posted for recruitment, and may not be the best source of information on what the real trends are in the industry.

You also need to bear in mind that recruiters tend to see things from a business leader perspective. That means they usually see things from the perspective of what the client thinks he wants to see, and not what may be most important for you to know.

Use caution when using a recruiter as your main source of information about job seeking. Some of them are quite bright and well informed, and can be very helpful. Others are as dumb as a post, and may be prone to providing you misleading information. (We addressed this topic a little when we spoke about résumés.)

Should a recruiter contact you, however, you should do your best to comply with his or her requests. A recruiter typically does not contact you just to pass the time of day, and if you are called it is because you match something they are trying to fill. So be nice to them! In this case they may actually be able to help you.

A good recruiter will be able to provide specific information on the company that is doing the hiring and on the position you are being considered for. One who is worth his or her salt will also brief you before each interview and provide what assistance he can to ensure you are the most competitive candidate in the heap. For this reason, working with a recruiter can be a decided advantage.

When a recruiter contacts you, it is because he wants to give you a boost over the wall into the interior of the castle of the lovely princess. Don't turn them down, but let them help you.

Chapter Ten

Creating a winning formula in your campaign

We have emphasized in this book that job seeking is not what a lot of people think it is. That being the case, understanding the game being played is important.

<u>The first thing to remember about job seeking is that it is a low percentage game.</u> This means there are many factors that can limit your ability to get the job you want. We have discussed some of these in this book. There are many forces at play to keep you from getting the job. Getting through all the obstacles is a daunting challenge, and you may have a number of opportunities slip past you before you finally land a good position.

In working sales, one does not expect to get a sale with every approach or with every opportunity. You will be rejected more often than you will be accepted. But a good salesman will expect to land one sale for every 10, 20 or 30 approaches.

With job seeking, the numbers are a lot worse! You may get passed by hundreds of times. With job seeking you may be out there fishing a very long time before you land what you want! You need to be prepared to deal with these numbers.

Although you could be fortunate enough to land something good early in your job campaign, this would be unusual. Perhaps your credentials are so good and there is such demand for what you have to offer that you do not have to be too concerned, and job seeking is more an aspect of choosing from among competing offers. If this is the case, you do not have to be particularly patient or persistent.

However, if job seeking were easy for you, you would not have picked up this book! Correct?

Thus for most people job seeking is typically not like sales when it comes to the numbers. You will not land an offer with every 20 approaches. It may take many hundreds, or well over a thousand approaches. The important thing to keep in mind is that you should not waste time and should keep trying to get in front of the right people as soon as you can.

A good salesman will get a sale between 5% to 20% of the time. With much job seeking activity the percent of success can be more like .005%. What you want to strive for is a success rate closer to .5% or maybe even 1%. These would be excellent numbers for a job seeking endeavour.

Don't be surprised if you encounter a lot of rejection. Rejection is the name of the game for a job seeker. Be prepared for it! Don't be discouraged and give up on good job seeking methods just because they do not bear fruit right away. Get your act together, do it right, and be persistent. Set a goal and focus on it. Don't give up until the fairy princess is yours!

A few things to bear in mind as you go assault your castle. First, the economy may have an impact on your efforts. If the economy is slow there may be a lot more resistance to your job seeking efforts from many departments. Of related consideration is the condition of your industry. If your industry is down, there will be fewer opportunities and a lot more competition for those opportunities that are available.

The second thing to bear in mind is that if you are implementing a major change in your career, you can anticipate reduced income. You will be dealing with a lot of resistance from employers who want experience in their industry. This means, if you are changing industries, you will not encounter as great a demand for your skills, so you may be obliged to reduce your compensation expectations to land a position.

In addition, if you are moving to a different area you may have difficulty getting the right contacts. You may also lack an understanding of the local economy, and in some cases there are regional culture differences you will be dealing with. If you are moving to a new area to look for a job you need to be prepared for losing some time in the process. You may have to scale a few walls to get where you are going.

The next principle is working with people. We talked earlier about "people-charging" your campaign. There are two basic aspects to this. The first is being able to work successfully with people you already know. The second is learning to get to know the people you need to get to know. Both aspects of working with contacts are vital to your success.

You need to know how to approach people without imposing on them by asking them to get you a job, but need to use your contact time asking for referrals to other people. Remember, when approaching people, whether you already know them or not, never ask for a job! Just ask for information and referrals.

Related to this concept, you need to bear in mind that the people who can help you the most are not necessarily the ones doing the hiring. In fact it would be rare if that were the case. The ones who can help you the most are the people who have the best connections. They will typically do a lot more for you than someone who has an opening. You may never qualify for an opening someone might have. But you can use your contact list to springboard you in front of someone who likes you well enough to bring you on board, even though he or she has no official openings this week.

Lastly, as you go out to contact people you know, or meet people you don't, or while you are developing your contact list, you will need to work on building a trust relationship with them. So much of today's business is based on trust relationships that you cannot hope to be truly successful until you have employed all of your efforts to establish trust with both the people you know as well as the people you meet.

To do this you need to determine (usually by simply asking them about it) what the principal focus of their business is, and what they need in the people who will be working for them. Show an interest in them as people and in their business. Asking them intelligent questions, and truly listening, their inputs can be invaluable. Build rapport, then build their trust by showing them you know what you are talking about but are always willing to listen.

In summary, here are some things to keep in mind that we have now discussed:

Remember to people-charge your campaign by working with key contacts and others who know you. Build your rolodex with the names of people you need to know in your industry, or people who are well connected. Focus on getting in front of these people and talking with them, not circulating résumés, or waiting for the mailman to bring you a job!

In correspondence, be crisp not wordy. Omit cover letters whenever possible, and keep your résumé to a readable length. Six page résumés are the kiss of death. If you can't get down to less than three pages, start over. In your document, be sure to cite numbers. Use email to follow up on previous meetings, not to initiate contact with someone.

In interviewing, capture your performance for the interviewer with good, well cropped story-examples. Cite numbers here also. Always make an effort to negotiate salary and conditions, but don't attempt to do so until you have the offer in front of you.

Please bear in mind that in job seeking, even if you do everything right you could still miss out, often for reasons far beyond your control!

One final word here. Make sure you are using your time wisely, and do not give up easily. Establish your goals and keep your focus on them. Be persistent. Do not let discouragement catch you! Stay busy doing the smart things, and remain vigilant in keeping your attitude positive.

In this vein it will be helpful to conduct a weekly evaluation of your campaign and your efforts. Have others who are competent in this endeavor work with you on this. Listen to those who know you well, and pay attention to those who know what they are talking about.

Read this book and carry it around with you. Refer to it often. It is designed to make you more productive in your career change. You will win more battles that way, and avoid a lot of pitfalls.

Now here is a summary of things to do and things to not do in your job search campaign. First the Don'ts.

>1. Don't waste time filling out job applications. Wait until you have the interview before filling it out.

>2. Don't waste time with cover letters. They intervene between the reader and the résumé, they exhaust a great deal of time and energy, and they are not needed in most cases anyway.

3. Don't waste time sending out unsolicited résumés via mail or email. If your stuff goes into the company in an envelope, or in an unsolicited email, it will not get the attention it deserves, and you have just wasted a lot of valuable time and energy.

4. Don't waste time contacting recruiters. Unless you have expertise in the industry or function this recruiter specializes in he or she will not waste their precious time messing with it.

5. Don't use "résumé paper". It is antiquated and dates you. The industry standard these days is bright white bond paper. (The thick stuff also costs more money than regular paper.)

6. Don't use poor networking techniques, wherein you assault your friends and relatives with a request for a job.

7. Don't be discouraged by the low percentage nature of this business. Remember you can be doing everything right but still not get a job.

Here are some things you should be doing:

1. Develop a plan of action for your campaign, including how you are going to tackle difficult problems, and how you are going to spend your time and energy.

2. Concentrate on using the Internet, and doing direct mail using a quality business letter.

3. Employ effective networking techniques to get attention, never asking for a job, but instead requesting advice and information. Use LinkedIn and other sources to identify people to approach.

4. Review good interviewing and negotiating techniques and employ them conscientiously.

5. Keep at it until you have scaled the castle wall and found your fairy princess. It is worth the effort.

One advantage of job seeking, you only have to close one sale to conclude the campaign. Although you are dealing with low percentages no matter what techniques you are applying, you only have one fairy princess to kiss. Keep going until you have that one sale – until you have assaulted the fairy castle and secured the regal maiden as yours.

When you land the job you want, write me a short letter. I would be pleased to hear from you.

Appendix One

Effective versus ineffective job seeking activities

This section reviews the less effective ways of job seeking and compares them against more effective methods. There is a value ascribed to each activity, which rates the effectiveness of this method against other methods. The lower the value the less effective the activity. The least effective methods are listed first. A brief explanation is provided of why this activity is more or less effective.

Value Activity

0.001 Filling out applications before you have been interviewed, or before you know for sure you have the qualifications for the job you would be considered for. Remember, applications are designed by the company for screening purposes in order to make it easier for them to screen you out. So the applications you are so carefully filling out will soon be used to turn you away! Don't fall for this. Get the interview first then fill out the application. Do not labor over a document unless you are confident the effort will bear fruit. If a company will not accept a résumé en lieu of an application then don't waste your time with them. The likelihood of them hiring you from your application alone is lower than ground level and is probably the least effective job seeking activity you can engage in.

0.005 Sending unsolicited résumés to companies with a cover letter. The cover letter gets in the way of the résumé and reduces its effectiveness. Preparing the cover letter absorbs a great deal of time and energy that should be devoted to more effective job seeking methods. The cover letter does very little for you and is mostly a waste of time. Wasting time in a fruitless activity is not advised. You should only use a cover letter if you are applying for a specific opening, you know the person you are addressing the résumé to, or if you have been referred for a position by someone the hiring manager or a company executive knows.

0.010 Sending unsolicited résumés or solicitations to recruiters. The chances of this landing in the right hands when you need it to are extremely small.

Unless this recruiter is recruiting in your industry and has a position he or she is trying to fill right now, your résumé will not result in anything any time soon. Sending a résumé to recruiters is something you can do when you do not need a job. That way they can load it in their database, and if a miracle happens they might call you someday. Remember the recruiters are only focusing on the most qualified people. If you are well qualified you may not need a recruiter to help you find a good job.

0.015 Sending unsolicited résumés to companies without a cover letter. Sending an unsolicited résumé is one of the least effective job seeking methods. But sometimes it works. Just don't hold out a lot of hope. You improve your chances by starting with an up to date list of companies in your industry.

0.02 Responding to openings listed in written or published media. You are competing against a lot of people and it takes a lot of time and energy to prepare a cover letter and get the stuff mailed (snail mail is old fashioned.) Not to mention the high cost of postage. You should only do this if you are a perfect match for the position and it appears they actually intend to fill the position.

0.025 Sending unsolicited emails. Email is a great follow up tool if you have already spoken with someone about a position, but is a terrible first approach method. Spam filters will pick you up quickly, and your electronic gem will be bashed or rerouted into oblivion. Another difficulty with this approach is being able to develop a good list of people to approach together with their email addresses (which could cost you a bundle.) The advantage of using email is it could take you less time to achieve contact with a lot of people. It is just very inefficient.

0.03 Responding to job openings listed on company websites on the Internet. Sometimes company job postings will have an easy application process which could save you time. The problem is they usually require you to complete a laborious online application which itself makes it much harder for you to gain admittance to their fairy castle. You should weigh the amount of effort to be expended on this activity against possible returns, which are usually pretty low. Other methods are likely more effective.

0.04 Ineffective networking. This is where you ask your friend or acquaintances about a job. The reason this is low on our list is because this method is often counterproductive, as you usually end up alienating friends, relatives or acquaintances. Remember, in networking you must never ask for a job, just for advice and information.

Note: None of the above job seeking activities are recommended, as they are mostly unproductive. Some people may land a job doing them, but for most people the chances are small.

The following activities are recommended things to do for most job seekers.

0.10 Responding to opening on job boards. Even though this activity is a very low percentage activity, it nevertheless takes very little time to do, because in most cases you can apply for a job with a few clicks of the mouse. This means you expend little time and energy doing so. You merely need to post your résumé on the job board, then when finding a job listing that interests you, you push the "apply" button. So this is a recommended activity, as long as it is not the only thing you are doing to find a job.

0.11 Posting your résumé on job boards. This is not as effective as other methods, but it is a passive activity involving less effort. What I mean is, once you have the résumé posted, you do not need to expend a lot of energy on the activity because interested parties will come to you. So this is an important activity to engage in. You should, however, freshen the résumé by making minute changes to the document every 10 to 12 days to make sure your résumé sits higher in the list of prospective candidates.

0.12 Creating a profile on LinkedIn. This activity is similar to posting to job boards, because you get broad exposure. Your profile will tend to be reviewed by all types of people in your industry and elsewhere. You should include your phone and email address on the profile so if someone is interested in you they can track you down. You should make it known when you create the profile you are job seeking. You can also post to other professional networking sites.

0.2 Sending stand alone (hard copy) letters to the leaders of key companies in your industry, or field of endeavor, asking for a chance to speak with them. There are various ways to identify who you might send these to. One very good method is by tapping LinkedIn for contacts. After your approach via letter, you should follow up with each person, and ask the targeted leader either for a networking meeting (informational interview) or a job interview. If this person is not in your locality, you should plan on having these discussions either by phone or Skype.

0.5 Effectively networking (not asking for a job, etc.) with association leaders, political leaders, religious leaders, alumni associations, chambers of commerce or other institutions. You are seeking information and advice. Gathering this information will lead you to real job openings with companies that are actually hiring. (This is the source of the fabled "hidden job market.")

1.0 Effectively networking with personal acquaintances or relatives. These people will traditionally give you more of their time than people you do not know yet.

2.0 Effectively networking (people charging) with business contacts outside or on the fringes of your primary industry or function, or in a secondary one. This is not as effective as networking your primary industry or function, but it is one of the most effective job seeking activities you can engage in.

3.0 Effectively networking with contacts in your primary industry or job function. Personal contacts should be first, then secondary contacts. With this activity you are operating at the edge of the castle wall, or near the main gate to the fabled city. So it will be easier to get inside. **This is most likely your most effective job seeking activity.**

Remember, with job seeking <u>anything you do is a relatively low percentage</u>. This means you will experience heavy rejection, <u>even if you are doing everything right</u> and using a high probability job seeking activity. Just keep up with the high productivity stuff. You must always concentrate on those activities most likely to generate employment, leaving the less productive methods to everyone who is not going to read this book.

Appendix Two

Addressing liabilities

Any candidate could carry liabilities that make it harder to get a job. There are also things called perceived liabilities.

Some liabilities are extremely hard to overcome, others can be covered up or shuffled to the background, while others can be mitigated. As mentioned before, since candidate selection is a matter of eliminating candidates until one finds the least objectionable, having a visible liability in some cases can be a severe handicap to job seeking. I will categorize a few of these below.

You can usually overcome secondary liabilities, or ones of a lesser degree, by employing effective job seeking methods, developing a well honed résumé, and by interviewing well. You can also mitigate certain liabilities by addressing them effectively. Naturally if you are using effective networking techniques you may be able to bypass the issue of your actual or perceived liabilities altogether.

If you have a primary (or serious) liability and you are seeking a job in a down economy, you can anticipate <u>severe difficulties</u> in landing a decent job, and need to be prepared for the economic conditions and their result. There are some career consulting companies that tout their ability to help you overcome these major liabilities, but their methods are pretty feeble when it comes to the daunting task of facing the job market carrying a ball and chain. In most cases having a serious liability is a legitimate cause for concern and cannot be ignored.

Here are some of those serious liabilities, and some things that can address or mitigate them.

Serious (Primary) Liabilities

1. Not having a proper work visa for the country you live in. If you are a professional, sometimes employers will sponsor you for a work visa. Some people can get by with this by paying someone to give them false papers, but this is not recommended. If you are not married, the easiest

way to get a work visa in most countries is to marry a citizen. Otherwise, good luck!

2. A felony or jail time. If you have been convicted of a felony or have spent more than a couple months in jail, you have a major problem. Some companies will not allow you to have any amount of jail time to be considered for a position. Other companies may be more flexible, much depending upon the type of job you are being considered for.

For most positions you will want to find creative ways of burying missed work periods on your résumé, and you will want to avoid completing an application until after you have a job offer. If you are convincing enough in your interview, and the nature of your offense is not too grievous, you may be able to get in the door despite the obstacles. You will want to concentrate on effective networking to identify opportunities where you will get due consideration before they delve too deeply into your background.

There are a surprising number of people in this country who have spent more than a little bit of time in jail. So having a conviction in your background is not necessarily fatal, but it is definitely problematic.

3. Not being able to speak English or the language of the country in which you are trying to get the job. If this is your problem, you need to figure out how you are going to get past the interview. For some positions English is not a requirement, but not being able to speak English (or whatever the primary language of your country of employment is) will be a severe impediment. Try some crash courses, and get help from people who can assist with the vocabulary of the job you are seeking. Some jobs do not require much language proficiency, but typically they do not pay that much.

4. If you are in poor health, or are over the hill in regards to age, or are suffering from a disability, you are facing an uphill battle if seeking a job. The same goes if you are pregnant or give the appearance of someone who may become pregnant. I realize it is wrong for employers to discriminate based on age, disability or other conditions, but this happens all the time. To beat this one you may wish to disguise your disability or condition the best you can. To address possible concerns about your age or health condition, you should show vigor in your step, and energy in everything you do.

Also, if they perceive you may abuse drugs or alcohol you will encounter significant resistance from the hiring authority. To address this, make sure you look real crisp when you show up for an interview, and make sure they do not smell evidence of your addiction. Then give up the addiction or you will probably lose the job anyway.

5. Lack of qualifications in your industry or function. This means a lack of experience or background that is needed for the job or jobs you might be considered for. This can be a serious liability. Your résumé will likely flag your limitations and make it hard for you to get due consideration. You should work on using good stand alone approach letters in order to avoid having to present a résumé until after you have had a successful interview.

6. Lack of educational qualifications or certification in your field. In some cases this can limit you significantly. You should concentrate on good networking technique, and avoid presenting a résumé or completing an application until after a successful interview.

7. Education is in the wrong area or field, or does not match the requirements of the job. Same approaches as above would apply. Where

possible you should omit the mismatched education from your résumé.

8. Fired for cause. This does not have to be the end of the world, because a lot of people get fired these days. But you will want to develop a good explanation for your termination without being too negative about your former employer. Once again good interview technique will help you avoid certain issues, and deferring completion of an application will be important here.

Secondary liabilities:

9. Bad references. This means you have people in the industry who do not like you, or think you are not good at what you do, and they pass the word. If the people who are doing this have enough contacts you can become a pariah with no ability to fix the problem. This greatly complicates the problems you have in seeking employment, especially if you are working in a small or highly specialized field.

10. Too much education. If you have a PhD and a Bachelors is required, or you have a degree but you are applying for a blue collar position, you might wish to omit the unnecessary education on your résumé, or suppress it on your

application. The problem here is that the employer will realize they will need to pay you more for what you do. So they will not want to hire you unless they have no other choice. So just don't let them know about the sheepskin until after you have a job.

11. Work history has you serving outside your field, industry or specialty. (For example, you are an engineer, but you worked as a school teacher for a few years in the middle of your career.) In this case you will want to devote less of your résumé to the area that does not support the type of job you are seeking. You should only mention this work in passing, and instead focus the résumé or application on the work you did that is applicable to the type of job you are applying for. If it is possible to do so without showing a gap in your employment history, you may want to omit the unsupportive experience from your résumé. Once again, avoid submitting an application until after you have interviewed successfully.

Other secondary liabilities could include such things as living in the wrong area, not interviewing well, not having a well written résumé, having a gap in your employment history, having a poor wage earnings record (lower salary than others with your experience) not being as effective or skilled at your job as others, education in a lesser known or less respected institution, having a foreign sounding name, speaking with an accent, having a dissimilar cultural background, etc.

Many of these liabilities can be addressed or mitigated with a well prepared résumé and good interview techniques. Others may require training or assistance. The key is to know in advance that you have a liability, or a perceived liability, recognize what the liability is and be prepared to address it. Depending upon your career specialty or industry, some of these can be more problematic than others. You should develop appropriate strategies for each type of liability you believe you have, and be prepared to apply them at the appropriate stage of your job search.

Don't become discouraged if you have a secondary liability. Most people in the job market have liabilities that can limit their competitiveness. You just have to work with it and press forward.

Please note that the biggest liability of all may be a self imposed one. That is your unwillingness to relocate. Relocation may be necessary for many jobs, and not giving it adequate consideration can severely limit your career choices. If you are serious about your career or about having a job versus not having one, then you need to focus on getting the job no matter where it is geographically, and relegate alternate considerations to the trash bin.

Some people object to relocation because their spouse is unwilling to do so. Even though family considerations for most people trump other considerations, having a decent job can greatly enhance your quality of life and your family situation.

If you are the primary breadwinner in your family the job needs to be of supreme importance to your family, as it is crucial to your condition now and in the future. If your spouse does not comprehend this then you may have some significant problems with your marriage. But that is a different subject.

www.ingramcontent.com/pod-product-compliance
Lightning Source LLC
Chambersburg PA
CBHW061509180526
45171CB00001B/108